CORRECTIONAL OFFICERS IN AMERICA

CORRECTIONAL OFFICERS IN AMERICA
The Emergence of a New Profession

Stephen Walters
and
Tom Caywood

The Edwin Mellen Press
Lewiston•Queenston•Lampeter

Jarrett Library
East Texas Baptist University
␣␣␣rshall, TX

Library of Congress Cataloging-in-Publication Data

Walters, Stephen.
    Correctional officers in America : the emergence of a new profession / Stephen Walters
and Tom Caywood.
        p. cm.
    Includes bibliographical references and index.
    ISBN-13: 978-0-7734-5717-1
    ISBN-10: 0-7734-5717-8
    1. Correctional personnel--United States. 2. Prisons--United States--Officials and
employees. 3. Prison administration--United States--History. I. Caywood, Tom. II. Title.

HV9470.W 2006

                                                                        2006049431

hors série.

A CIP catalog record for this book is available from the British Library.

Copyright © 2006 Stephen Walters and Tom Caywood

All rights reserved. For information contact

                The Edwin Mellen Press   The Edwin Mellen Press
                        Box 450   Box 67
                Lewiston, New York   Queenston, Ontario
                USA 14092-0450   CANADA L0S 1L0

                        The Edwin Mellen Press, Ltd.
                        Lampeter, Ceredigion, Wales
                        UNITED KINGDOM SA48 8LT

                Printed in the United States of America

H V
9470
.W35
2006

BOT

#||

3-08

to Kelisen and Donna
sw

to my wife Lana, my sons Eli and Nathan, and my mother and brothers.
tc

TABLE OF CONTENTS

LIST OF ILLUSTRATIONS

TABLES

FIGURES

FOREWORD

The world of corrections is vastly unrecognized. Corrections is pervasive in almost all societies. Little is known about corrections among the general population, and the mere mention of the term has no significance for most citizens. Yet corrections is expected to correct those who eventually are processed by the vast criminal justice system. Every convicted criminal offender will have contact with some aspect of corrections at one time or another. The nature of such contact may be intense or intermittent and infrequent. The clientele are immensely diverse.

Corrections consists of the large aggregate of organizations, agencies, and personnel who supervise and oversee those convicted of crimes. Local, state, and federal corrections are represented as a massive, collective effort to exercise some degree of control over 8 million or more criminals and others. In 2006, over 2 million offenders were in institutions known as prisons and jails. The remainder comprised the majority of the supervised population known categorically as community corrections clients. Institutionalized offenders are inmates, while those in community corrections are considered as clients. Two thirds of these clients are probationers, while the remainder are parolees, work/study releasees, furloughees, and divertees.

To a degree, the invisibility of corrections in American society is self-imposed. Prisons are most likely located in remote rural areas or places not generally frequented. Jails are often situated in city centers, and they are difficult to detect unless someone is looking specifically for them. Community correctional organizations and activities are even more transparent. For rehabilitative and reintegrative purposes, it is important that supervised clients blend into the social fabric of their communities. For many citizens, the idea of "out of sight, out of mind" pertains aptly to corrections. Their usefulness and functions are acknowledged, but most people are content with the blissful ignorance of not knowing where correctional organizations are and/or the specific identities and whereabouts of most correctional clients.

When celebrities or other high-profile persons commit crimes or get into trouble, we have a general idea of what happens to them through their trials, but not much is known about what happens beyond such proceedings. The media keeps track of crimes, particularly sensational ones, and the public is kept informed of the investigative efforts of police relating to these crimes. When certain crimes are solved and perpetrators are subsequently convicted, our memories of these events fade and are replaced by new sensationalized crimes and suspects. Follow-ups of these previously sensationalized events are infrequent. Little or nothing is known about the status of most criminal offenders in the aftermath of their trials and punishments.

These preliminary observations about corrections are a prelude to this book, which focuses on the personnel who comprise this vast field. Like corrections, those persons who work in different capacities with inmates and clients perform very important roles. They work directly with those insulated from us: prisoners, probationers, and parolees. Correctional personnel considered as an aggregate often go about their work without much attention or recognition from their communities. More often than not, the work they perform goes unrecognized and unrewarded, a continuing series of thankless tasks performed. However, these persons must acquire numerous skills and possess special knowledge in order to be effective. Their motives for seeking to work in the correctional field are diverse. But they all share several common characteristics.

They want to help others who society shuns. They want to make a difference in the lives of those who have broken the law. They want to make the world a better place through the work they perform. They are committed to social improvement in a variety of ways. Their work requires patience, strength, dedication, a strong moral sense, and the flexibility and ingenuity to cope with those who often reject them or are resistant to their well-intentioned interventions.

Stephen Walters and Tom Caywood have provided us with a rare glimpse into the world of correctional officers in both institutional and community corrections. This work is unique because few studies of the intricacies of correctional work have been published. Furthermore, compared with other investigations of this profession, few writers have had the skills and expertise reflected by these authors to describe in rich detail the nature of correctional work. Both authors have immersed themselves in the correctional field for decades. They have conducted many investigations of correctional officers from numerous jurisdictions. Their analysis and description of correctional officers is couched in the context of over 40 combined years of work with all types of officers, through interviews, observation, questionnaires, and other data-gathering strategies. Thus, their work fills a void that needs to be filled. And it succeeds superbly.

Walters and Caywood describe their work as an analysis of the occupational environment of correctional officers. Not only do they describe this environment in enriching detail, but they embellish their description with true versions of what actually transpires, dispelling various myths which have evolved over the years about the work of prison guards. But this work extends far beyond a mere description of the people who work in corrections and what they do. This book describes the entire social and interpersonal contextual environment of officers, including the continuing problems they must confront, their modes of coping with these problems, and nature of their interactions with both inmates and clients. This work is comprehensive in that it depicts the lives of those who work not only in prisons, but others who work in communities to rehabilitate and reform criminals.

The organization of the book is both logical and sound. It begins with placing corrections in the larger mosaic of the criminal justice system. An historical perspective about the evolution of corrections is presented, with a focus upon early prison and correctional developments and events. The philosophical bases of corrections are presented, and we are able to trace easily the gradual transformation of the correctional field from its rudimentary beginnings to its more contemporary forms.

These authors move easily from the historical antecedents of corrections to the selection and training of correctional personnel. Over the centuries, the profession of corrections has undergone a substantial metamorphosis, where today officers who work with offenders are well-trained, educated, and capable. The process of selection and training corrections officers is described, including the contemporaneous professionalism of regional and national organizations which have formed and evolved to facilitate such developments.

All levels of corrections are described, including federal, state, and local levels. Correctional officers are described, including their training, the work they perform, and the persons they supervise. Depending upon the different working environments of correctional officers, special skills are required to supervise offenders effectively. The social dynamics of correctional settings of all types are examined in great detail. We learn much about how correctional officers do their jobs and put their skills to use. All correctional work is done also in an increasingly legalistic environment, where inmate and client rights have been acquired. Thus, greater educational requirements have accompanied one's training as a corrections officer, in order that all parties operate in their respective environments mutually respecting the legal rights they have acquired.

Walters and Caywood describe the personal stresses of correctional work. Accompanying this work is stress, which manifests itself in various forms. Corrections populations are dangerous, both inside and outside of prison or jail walls. Thus, more than a few officers experience burnout in the course of performing their jobs. Some officers become cynical about their work and the input they exert which influences the lives of those they supervise. The social psychology of correctional officers is described, including different outcomes of stress and burnout. Personal adaptations to job stressors are explained. One adaptation to work stress is the creation of an officer subculture, where common values and ideas are shared. It has been said that every organization has a formal component, but that informal social organization inevitably emerges. This is true of correctional environments, and these authors examine the subculture of correctional officers. We are taken behind the scenes to see this subculture in the most up close and personal ways.

These authors would be remiss if they failed to describe the important and growing role of minorities as correctional officers. They have not disappointed us here. Much attention is given to the growing presence of minority officers in the performance of corrections tasks. Minorities, particularly women and persons of different races and ethnicities, have a significant presence in correctional work. In earlier times in American history, women and minorities were virtually nonexistent in correctional roles. But times have changed. Today a significant proportion of the correctional work force exhibits considerable gender, racial, and ethnic diversity. The important roles performed by minorities are described in depth.

Beyond prison walls exists a vast correctional component existing in all American communities. Community corrections comprises over two thirds of the corrections field. Walters and Caywood have provided us with a complete description of this correctional work force as well. Probation and parole officers must oversee a portion of the criminal element as well, but outside of prison walls. Persons on probation and parole are supervised more or less intensively, and these types of corrections officers are charged with monitoring them effectively. There are several important contrasts between what probation and parole officers do on the one hand, and what correctional officers do in institutional settings on the other. These contrasts are discussed. Walters and Caywood present a typology of these officers which acquaints us with the many different approaches these personnel use in their officer-client interactions.

This book concludes appropriately with a discussion of several salient correctional issues. These issues touch upon various sensitive areas, such as prison privatization and unionization of officers. Not everyone is enamored with the idea of private corrections, although it is a growing and increasingly important part of both institutional and community corrections. The pros and cons of privatization are elaborated. Also, various diseases, such as AIDS/HIV and tuberculosis, have become increasingly prevalent among offender populations. Special care must be exercised by officers when dealing with increasingly numbers of infected offenders. The risks posed to officers by these offenders are described, and different methods for isolating and segregating these offenders from the general inmate population have been described.

Prisons are violent places. More often than we realize, there are incidents involving inmates where force must be used to control them. Whether these incidents are riots or simply noncompliant inmates, the use of force by correctional officers becomes necessary. Thus both violence and the force necessary to quell it are depicted. A legalistic foundation for this issue is presented. Last but not least, these authors address the issue of professionalization. The American Correctional Association, the American Jail Association, and the American Probation and Parole Association have taken official positions on the professionalization issue, and each organization has evolved standards by which officers can carry out their work in ideal ways. The accreditation and professionalization processes are discussed, and the importance of professionalization is underscored.

This book is a strong and important contribution to the existing literature in the correctional field. It describes, educates, and informs. It's reading is a must for those seeking to learn more about the profession of corrections, especially for those interested in pursuing correctional careers. Whether it is used as a stand-alone book for a course about corrections officers or a companion piece for a standard textbook in the field, this work is remarkable and unique for the great detail it provides about corrections officers.

Dean John Champion
Texas A & M International University
Laredo, TX

ACKNOWLEDGEMENTS

I would like to thank my co-author Tom Caywood, my colleagues Drs. Dean Champion, Beau Duncan, Roberto Heredia, and Mohamed Ben-Ruwin, and our reviewers Drs. Fran Reddington and Betsy Witt.

Stephen Walters
University of Houston - Clear Lake

I would like to thank my department chair Joe Lomax for his support in writing this book. I would also like to thank Ed Ross for his contributions, and Cheryl Fuller, Susan Hilal, Kathy Winz, Aric Dutelle, and Dale Kapla for their support. Finally, I thank Stephen Walters for allowing me to become involved in this project, and our reviewers Drs. Fran Reddington and Betsy Witt.

Tom Caywood
University of Wisconsin - Platteville

1

THE WORLD OF CORRECTIONAL OFFICERS

While discussions of crime, criminals, and the police have long fascinated professionals and laymen alike, prisons, and those who maintain order within their walls, have generally been ignored, misunderstood, or in some cases vilified. This is perhaps natural, as prisons have historically been isolated entities, intentionally cut off from society and the outside world.

One of the first social scientists to examine the uniqueness of correctional institutions, and their affects upon the inhabitants, was Erving Goffman. His classic analysis *Asylums* (1961) identified prisons as a type of *total institution*, which he defined as

> ....a place of residence and work where a large number of like-situated individuals, cut off from society for an appreciable amount of time, lead together an enclosed, formally administered round of life. (Prisons serve as a clear example...) (Goffman, 1961: xxiii).

Thus the uniqueness of prisons, and the complex social environment that develops within them, largely escaped notice of both criminologists and society in general. While inmates were at times eagerly examined by social scientists, the "guards" or *correctional officers* ("COs") were for the most part ignored.

This book is an analysis of correctional officers, whether employed as a civilian jailer or a commissioned officer in a city or county jail, an officer with a state's department of corrections, or a member of the Federal Bureau of Prisons. This text will focus on the role of the almost a quarter of a million correctional officers responsible for supervising over two million inmates nationwide - 1.3 million in prisons, and another 690,000 in jails.

Organization of the Book

Correctional officers are affected by the environment in which they function. This environment not only includes the immediate physical prison surroundings, but also the professional/legal system in which corrections, as a functional entity, must interrelate. Accordingly, this research begins with an overview of the criminal justice system and how the field of corrections relates to the other components. Additionally a brief history of corrections and correctional philosophy is presented with an emphasis upon changes in the role of the correctional officer.

Chapters 2 and 3 continue the exploration of structural factors affecting the correctional officer force. Examined are the history and evolution of correctional officers as a profession, and understanding how and why people become correctional officers, including the selection and training process one must complete to become a correctional officer. The demographic characteristics of correctional officers are observed, and how such characteristics as age, education, length of experience, rank and geographic location affect a correctional officer's attitudes are also explored.

The second section of the book, including chapters 4, 5, 6 and 7 examines some of the interpersonal aspects of being a CO. The balance between maintaining institutional security and the rigors associated with that task and respecting the basic human rights and dignities of inmates can be an arduous undertaking. Chapter four examines the relationship between the keepers and the kept. This chapter explores how correctional officers find ways to ensure compliance from inmates without resorting to coercive power. Variations in officers attitudes and behaviors are examined in depth. Research shows that just like police officers, correctional officers develop working personalities.

Chapter 5 covers the social psychology of correctional officers. Correctional officers are in constant conflict with two different but equally important groups: inmates and administrators. Both groups contribute to numerous social psychological difficulties which are encountered by correctional officers throughout their careers. These difficulties can include feelings of stress, burnout, alienation, role conflict, cynicism, and job dissatisfaction. This chapter also reviews administrative practices which helps ameliorate these problems.

Chapter 6 delves into the subculture of correctional officers. It explains how correctional officers view their professional world. Various typologies are reviewed to explain officer behavior and the different phases of an officer's career. The world of correctional officers is examined through the officer subculture. An informal correctional officer "code" provides a blueprint for officers working in a difficult and often hostile environment. Understanding this unwritten set of shared assumptions about how correctional officers should act on the job is essential for understanding their behavior.

Chapter 7 examines the role of women and minorities in the correctional field. While still a predominately white male career field, great efforts have been made over the last thirty years to diversify the correctional officer corps. Prior to the 1970s, very few women and virtually no blacks worked as correctional officers. Title VII of the Civil Rights Act of 1964 and the 1972 amendments provided the legal context for diversifying the prison work force.

Chapter 8 focuses on a special type of correctional officer. Rather than functioning behind prison walls, *probation and parole officers* continue to supervise offenders in the community. Their unique activities and problems are explored.

The finally, Chapter 9 examines critical issues confronting the field of corrections: the unionization of correctional officers, the privatization of corrections, the risks of infectious diseases in the prison environment, violence and the use of force, the development of emergency response teams in prisons, and the "professionalization" of correctional officers   All are critical issues confronting correctional officers in the 21st century.

The Criminal Justice System

Correctional officers don't function in a vacuum, but rather can be viewed as specialized cogs in a complex American criminal justice machine. This system is a three-component, three-tiered system. The components are law enforcement, courts, and corrections. The tiers are local, state, and federal governments. Each component can be found at each tier, while each component has specific functions. Unlike many criminal justice systems worldwide, the criminal justice system in this country can be characterized as fragmented and localized. We are a nation of many separate and independent criminal justice agencies, all of which utilize correctional officers.

Local agencies are comprised of municipal and county officials. The bulk of the criminal justice system business is carried out at this level. There are over 12,000 police departments and over 3,000 sheriffs' departments in this country. Larger municipalities also have their own court and correctional systems, thus becoming their own self-contained, mini-criminal justice systems. Municipal judges hear cases presented by municipal prosecutors against offenders charged with violating city ordinances. Convictions result in fines and/or confinement in the municipal jail. Smaller municipalities and most counties rely on local court systems to dispense justice. Individuals arrested on state misdemeanor or state felony charges are generally tried locally (states are free to name their own courts, therefore specific names vary by state). These are courts of record. A police officer can arrest an individual either for violating a city ordinance (minor offense) or a state statute (more serious offense). A city ordinance violation would be tried in municipal court, and if convicted, the offender can be sentenced to serve time in either a city jail or the county jail. The workhorses of the criminal justice system are the trial courts of general jurisdiction. State misdemeanor and felony cases are tried at this level. Individuals convicted of misdemeanor offenses can be sentenced to serve their time in the county jail, while those individuals convicted of felonies are sentenced to serve time at a state correctional institution.

The second tier of the system is the state level. State law enforcement agencies include state police or highway patrol, state criminal investigators, fish and wildlife agencies, alcohol beverage control agencies and state tax collection agencies, to name a few. State court systems generally are three-tiered, with a trial court of general jurisdiction, intermediate appellate courts, and a court of last resort. At the local level, in trial courts of general jurisdiction, commonly only one judge sits on the bench to hear direct testimony, review items introduced into evidence, and hear oral arguments from the both state's attorney and the defendant's attorney. Jury trials are conducted at this level. Intermediate appellate courts, or the court of appeals, hear only cases in which the ruling of the lower court is challenged by one of the parties. No new evidence or new testimony is generally allowed as these courts only rule on points of law. Normally several judges form the appellate bench. They review the lower court's record and hear oral arguments by both sides. Courts of last resort are generally called state supreme courts, where multiple judges review lower court records, written briefs, and hear oral arguments. Appellate judges issue written opinions on the case. Judges at the state level can be appointed or elected, depending on how the system is set up in each state. In some states judges belong to political parties, in other states judges are elected in non-partisan elections and yet in others they are appointed by a political leader, usually the governor, and voters decide whether or not the judge should remain in office. Voters can then remove a judge appointed by the governor. This process serves as part of our system of checks and balances. State correctional institutions house the most serious and violent offenders convicted of violating state law. These institutions are generally classified as either minimum security, medium security or maximum security. In recent years, many states have built super maximum prisons to house the most violent offenders in that system. Correctional officers are employed by the state and can work at any of the state's correctional institutions. Probation and parole officers are generally part of the state's department of corrections. These officers supervise convicted offenders who are sentenced by a court to serve their sentence in the community.

The federal system is the upper tier of the criminal justice system, and functions to enforce federal law in America. There are over 50 law enforcement agencies at this level. Most are in the Department of Justice, the Department of Treasury, or the Department of Homeland Security. These agencies are responsible for enforcing federal laws. There are 94 district federal courts in the nation. They are the workhorses of the federal system. District courts are the trial courts of general jurisdiction at the federal level, and trials are overseen by a district court judge. There are 11 intermediate appellate courts at the federal level. Each court has a specific area of the country in which they hear appeals for the federal district courts located in that area. These courts are known as Federal Courts of Appeals or Federal Circuit Courts. The United States Supreme Court is the highest court in the land, and therefore the court of last resort. Nine justices sit on the Supreme Court. All federal judges are appointed by the President and confirmed by the senate. They are appointed for life. Federal prosecutors are appointed by the attorney general of the United States. The Federal Bureau of Prisons is tasked with housing all federal inmates. To fulfill this responsibility the national government maintains more than 100 correctional institutions throughout the country. Because of jurisdictional differences, the type of inmates found in the Federal Bureau of Prisons are markedly different than their state-controlled counterparts. These differences are shown in Table 1.1.

TABLE 1.1
FEDERAL AND STATE PRISON INMATES
1997/2001

	Drug*	Violence*	Property**	Other**
State	21%	49%	22%	10%
Federal	57%	10%	8%	15%

*Source: Bureau of Justice Statistics. (2005). *Criminal Offender Statistics*. Washington, D.C.: U.S. Department of Justice.

**Source: United States General Accounting Office. (2000). *State and Federal Prisoners*. Washington, DC: United States General Accounting Office.

Of all of these entities, law enforcement is the most visible component and corrections the least visible. Uniformed law enforcement officers bring the services of the criminal justice system to the public. They are the provider of services, the peace keepers, the law enforcers. The motto for many departments is to "protect and serve." They initiate the operation of the criminal justice system by arresting a person for violating the law. They are the catchers. Once an arrest is made an offender can be temporarily housed in a local jail that is operated by a police department or the sheriff's department while the offender is awaiting disposition by a court.

Courts are the most formally structured component of the system. The decorum of a courtroom provides a serious tone for the matter at hand: determining the guilt or innocence of the accused. The state's case rests on the evidence provided by law enforcement officers, victims and witnesses. The prosecutor is the state's advocate who provides the evidence and testimony to convince the jury of the offender's guilt. The defense attorney represents the defendant. The defense attorney's task is to cast enough doubt on the state's case by the introduction of evidence and testimony sufficient to sway the jury to return a verdict of not guilty. Ideally there is a formalized duel between the prosecutor and the defense, yet in reality about 90 percent of all cases are plea bargained. A deal is cut between the prosecutor and the defense and a costly, time-consuming trial is avoided.

The actors in the judicial system are the best educated of all the actors in the criminal justice system. Very few law enforcement agencies or correctional organizations require their employees to have a college degree. All lawyers and almost all judges are law school graduates who have passed a state bar examination. Many newly sworn judges receive special training in court room operations. In many jurisdiction in this country prosecutors and judges are elected officials.

In 2004 almost 6.9 million adult Americans were under some form of correctional custody. Over 3 percent of the adult population or 1 in every 32 American adults fell into this category. About a third are incarcerated with about 1.4 million in prison and about 714,000 in jails (DOJ, 2005). "The prison environment requires that the correctional officer function as a social control agent who has the primary responsibilities of custody, security and control" (Pollock, 1997: 10). As formal social control agents, correctional officers are responsible for supervising individuals found guilty by a court of law. These officers assist the state in its responsibility for punishing violators of the criminal code.

Interestingly, although the least visible and least glamorous component of the criminal justice system, corrections has more and longer contact with an offender than any other component of the criminal justice system. The police, the most visible component, are seen as the catchers. There are numerous television programs illustrating police work, but programs featuring COs are virtually non-existent. The popular drama series *Law and Order,* in its opening credits states that in the criminal justice system the people are represented by two groups - the police and the prosecution. No mention is made of the corrections component. Yet many of those arrested by law enforcement and who are awaiting trial will spend time in the county jail. The average length of time from arrest to sentencing in 1996 was 219 days, or slightly more than 7 months (Brown, Langan and Levin, 1999). For the small percentage of offenders who request a jury trial the average length of time from arrest to sentencing was 355 days, while for those who plead guilty the average length of time from arrest to sentencing was 235 days. In 1996, almost a million felons were convicted in state courts. Of those almost 70 percent were sentenced to a period of confinement, while the other 30 percent were sentenced to probation. Almost 40 percent of those sentenced were sentenced to state prisons while about 31 percent were sentenced to serve short term confinement in jails. The average sentence length for a felon in a local jail was 6 months, although the average sentence length in state prison was 62 months. The average sentence for a murderer is about 20 years, and about one in three murderers is sentenced for life. Only about 3 percent receive the death penalty (Brown, Langan and Levin, 1999). At the end of 2000, almost 3,600 prisoners were under a sentence of death. Those sentenced to death were in prison for an average of 11 years before they were executed. Of those sentenced to death, 85 were eventually executed in 2000 (Snell, 2001).

Regardless of which tier of the system employs correctional officers, whether local, state or federal, those individuals will be in contract with offenders for longer periods of time than any other agents in the criminal justice system. With mandatory sentencing, and "three strikes and you're out" laws, it is possible for correctional officers to spend their entire career working with the same inmates.

There are almost two million people employed in the justice system of America. Table 1.2 indicates almost half of all justice system employees work in law enforcement, about one in five work in the judicial and legal field, and the remaining one-third work in corrections.

TABLE 1.2
PERCENTAGE OF JUSTICE SYSTEM EMPLOYMENT
BY LEVEL OF GOVERNMENT AND ACTIVITY
2000

	Police	Judicial	Corrections	Total
Federal	10	11.9	4.4	8.6
State	9.9	33.4	63.4	32.3
Local	80.1	54.7	32.2	59.1

Source: Bureau of Justice Statistics. (2004). *Sourcebook of Criminal Justice Statistics, 2003.* Washington, D.C.: U.S. Department of Justice.

While law enforcement is a local responsibility, corrections is generally a state responsibility. Four out of five law enforcement personnel are employed by municipal or county governments, whereas almost two-thirds of all correctional employees work at the state level. These 400,000 personnel are responsible for supervising over 1.4 million offenders (see Table 1.3).

The Federal Bureau of Prisons (BOP), as of June 2000, was the second largest employer of federal officers with authority to carry firearms and make arrests. Over 13,000 federal correctional officers maintain security over 160,000 inmates at 102 institutions (Reaves and Hart, 2001; BOP Quick Facts, 2002).

TABLE 1.3
PERCENTAGE OF JUSTICE SYSTEM EXPENDITURES
BY LEVEL OF GOVERNMENT AND ACTIVITY 2000

	Police	Judicial	Corrections	Total
Federal	17.6	21.2	7.1	14.8
State	12.5	36.1	62.9	34.7
Local	70	42.7	30	50.5

Source: Bureau of Justice Statistics. (2004). *Sourcebook of Criminal Justice Statistics, 2003.* Washington, D.C.: U.S. Department of Justice.

The Development of Prisons

Incarceration of criminal offenders as a method of punishment is a relatively recent concept for mankind. Corporal punishment, such as standing in a pillory, branding, flogging, mutilation - or even death were common forms of punishment. Banishment and later transportation were other ways of punishing offenders. Jails, or gaols, were used primarily to hold offenders awaiting trial or as a debtors prison. These facilities were not designed to house long term prisoners and, like jails in modern day America, were under the control of a sheriff.

In the United States our modern prison system had its beginnings in the late eighteenth century. Prior to the Revolutionary War, as a British colony, British penalties were in force here in America, and corporal punishment was the predominant means of dispensing justice. Transportation was a common practice for the British to empty their jails of convicted offenders, and many were transported to America to serve out their time.

12

Early American Attempts

One of the first groups to address the treatment of inmates was the Philadelphia Society for Alleviating the Miseries for the Public Prisons. Benjamin Franklin and Benjamin Rush were among its most prominent members. The society called for an early classification system, which required the separation of offenders by age, sex, race and the severity of offenses. They were proponents of the isolation movement. The Quakers in Pennsylvania were instrumental in abolishing the death penalty in the 1780s. It was thought that inmates should be housed in individual cells with little or no contact with other inmates. Their only contact would be with officials of the institution, and then only rarely. America's earliest real attempt at a modern prison, the Walnut Street Jail, was expanded in 1790 to include 30 solitary cells (Ives, 1970). In isolation inmates would have an opportunity to reflect on their misdeeds. Although this institution was highly copied, their overuse and resulting overpopulation required some rethinking. Thus was the beginnings of the Pennsylvania System, or what was also known as the "separate system."

In the early nineteenth century two state penitentiaries in Pennsylvania were built, the Eastern State Penitentiary (Cherry Hill) near Philadelphia and the Western State Penitentiary near Pittsburgh. The *Pennsylvania System* featured solitary confinement and attempted to rehabilitate offenders through religious salvation. A rival system developed in New York state at about the same time. The *Auburn System* (or congregate system) had inmates working together but sleeping in solitary cells. While they could work and eat together they were forbidden to speak to fellow inmates. Inmate infractions were met with harsh discipline:

> Here, too, penance and purity were sought: solitary penance by night, pure labor by day, silence broken only by the sound of

machines and tools. Throughout, prisoners had time to reflect and repent. The congregate system retained the monastic features of the separate system, in its solitary cells and silent labor, but blended the with a more contemporary lifestyle. A monastery at night; by day, a quasi-military organization of activities (all scheduled), movement (in unison and in lockstep), eating (backs straight, at attention), and work (long hours, usually at rote factory labor). The aim of this system was to produce docile, obedient inmates....(Johnson, 1997· 31).

Both systems touted their own benefits and for years the debate continued. The Auburn system eventually became the model for American correctional institutions for a long period of time.

Early on in prison development it was realized that prisons were extremely expensive commodities. Attempts to utilize the inmates to defray some of the prison's costs were inevitable and by the turn of the Twentieth Century the *Industrial Prison* system arose. In these institutions several modalities were developed for the effective financial use of inmates. In the *lease system* inmates were given over to a local businessman or farmer for his utilization, normally with COs providing security Instead of being paid for their labor the inmates received nothing, but monies paid by their temporary employers went directly to the prison. The inmates were generally returned to the prison at day's end. In another form, the *contract system*, an employer would actually set up a factory within the prison walls, providing machinery, at which inmates would toil. Again the prison itself was the recipient of any inmate "wages", not the inmates themselves. A variation of this form, the *piece-price system*, involved an entrepreneur who would provide the prison with raw materials and buy back the finished product from the institution. Other revenue producing modalities were also developed. The *public use system* puts inmates to work profitably building state infrastructure, while the *state-use* system allowed inmates to produce goods to be used by governmental agencies. While all of these systems were profitable, they eventually succumbed to political pressure caused by the massive unemployment in America during the Depression.

Modern Prison Types

As noted earlier, American prisons are loosely categorized into three levels of security - minimum, medium, and maximum. It should be noted that these security levels encompass both *perimeter security* and *internal security* procedures. Maximum security prisons utilize high levels of both perimeter and internal security. Perimeter security in these prisons many times includes the use of walls to both keep inmates in and the outside world out. Walls, though very expensive, provide both a physical barrier between inmates and the civilian population, but also serve to more completely separate convicts psychologically from the outside world. These walls provide limited access to and egress from the institution, and will employ *sallyports* for this purpose. A sallyport is a two-door security entrance that requires that only one door be opened at a time, thus limiting the ability of inmates to escape through these portals. Walls are supplemented by guard towers, constantly staffed by armed COs, to maintain perimeter integrity. Further security methodologies may include perimeter patrols and electronic monitoring. Internal security in a maximum security prison is also high. Officer-controlled multiple cell locking devices, referred to as "racking" mechanisms, ensure that COs can quickly secure the institution. Movement by inmates into non-housing areas is restricted, and many times requires an accompanying correctional officer. Intensive supervision of inmates at all times is the norm, as is a limitation on the amount of personal possessions a inmate may have. Searches of inmates and their living areas, called "shakedowns", are frequent and extensive.

Medium security prisons feature moderate levels of perimeter and internal security. In these institutions the most common form of perimeter security is fencing. Whether single or double barrier, fences have been found to be an effective and less expensive alternative to walls. These fences utilize sallyports, and may be supplemented with a variety of electronic monitoring systems, including motion detectors. Guard towers are also employed, although not all may be manned at all times. Internal security is not as severe as in a maximum security prison. While limitations on inmate possessions remain, as do the practice of shakedowns, neither are as extensive or frequent. Inmate movement many times is controlled by a system of "zonal security", where inmates are allowed to enter certain defined areas of the institution unaccompanied, but are denied access to other defined zones. Correctional officers are, of course, responsible for cell locking, but single cell locking is more common than in maximum security. These institutions are where most rehabilitative efforts take place.

The lowest security level is minimum security. Perimeter security in these prisons is limited, comprised of fences, or non-existent. What keeps most inmates in these institutions is a pro-social correctional history, and the good sense to appreciate the benefits of these prisons vis-a-vis more secure correctional environments. Barracks housing or individual rooms are the normal accommodations. These prisons are many times organized around some economic activity, such as farming, ranching, or forestry. Inmate movement is therefore many times merely determined by work scheduling, and considerable freedom exists. These prison types are detailed in Table 1.4.

TABLE 1.4
SECURITY LEVELS OF AMERICAN PRISONS
2000

	Total	Federal	State	Private
	1668	84	1320	264
Maximum	332	11	317	4
Medium	522	29	428	65
Minimum	814	44	575	195

Source: Bureau of Justice Statistics. (2003). *Sourcebook of Criminal Justice Statistics, 2002.* Washington, D.C.: U.S. Department of Justice.

Correctional Philosophy

Not only has the structure of American corrections changed over the years, but so has the philosophical foundation upon which incarceration has rested. The earliest correctional philosophy might be termed *retaliation.* The point of this perspective was that justice was best served by "getting even" with the offender. At first the individual victim was tasked with obtaining justice in most cases, while later on society in general took over this duty. The operant concept in use was *lex talionis*, or "an eye for an eye". At first taken literally, later the concept evolved into our modern system of equating a period of incarceration proportionate to the crime. It was believed that punishing offenders would either stop them from committing further criminal acts (specific deterrence) or by making their punishment an example for others, serving as a warning for society (general deterrence). While this reliance on punishment might seem primitive to some, it served as the basis for the first scientific thinking about crime and punishment. This group of reformers came to be known as the Classical School of Criminology, and they believed that punishment was a practical methodology, but only if it could be shown that punishment provided some societal advantage.

As society evolved and attitudes changed, the goal of corrections changed to *reformation*. Here prisons would help offenders realize the errors of their ways, either through religious conversion (Pennsylvania System), or through the discipline of hard work (Auburn and Industrial Systems). This approach stressed individuals changing themselves for the better through the rigors of confinement.

Later, as both the medical and social sciences matured, their concepts and methodologies were imported into prisons. These new sciences gave rise to the ideals of *rehabilitation* - that outside intervention, be it psychological, sociological, or criminological - could effect change in inmates. Inmates would be "treated" until they were "cured" of their criminal tendencies. This approach, although falling on hard times of late, could be effective given proper inmate selection and appropriate institutional support.

With the perceived failure of rehabilitation, a new approach, addressing what was thought to be the failings of both punishment and rehabilitation, arose. Concerned not only with inmates but with all actors in the criminal justice system, the *justice* approach eschewed traditional correctional thinking and emphasized the provision of fairness and honesty in the incarceration process, not only for the incarcerated but also for their keepers.

The Working Environments of Correctional Officers

In 2002, there were over 435,000 state and federal correctional employees including administrative personnel, clerical, educational, professional/technical, maintenance and food services and custodial. Almost two thirds of all state and about two-fifths of federal correctional employees (255,860) are classified as custody or security occupations (Camp, 2003). The larger percentage of correctional officers at the state level is attributed to the larger number of violent offenders in the system (Bureau of Justice Statistics, 1997). These employees are located in over 1375 state and 125 federal facilities. The majority at both levels work in minimum security facilities housing fewer than 500 inmates - not the typical image of correctional officers working in the "big house."

At the county level, most offenders are housed by the sheriff's office in county jails. Over 290,000 sworn and civilian personnel are employed by the 3,088 sheriffs agencies in this country. Nationwide, about 31 percent (58,000) of the nearly 200,000 sworn deputies are in jail-related positions. The percentage can vary greatly by agency. In Los Angeles County, the largest sheriff's department in the country, about 26 percent of the 8,000 plus deputies are involved in jail operations. Cook County (Chicago), Illinois, on the other hand has about 58 percent of its 5,800 deputies involved in jail related activities. In Suffolk County, Massachusetts, almost all of its 800+ sworn personnel are engaged in jail operation. As a cost-saving factor many county agencies are civilianizing many aspects of the job. Civilian dispatchers and civilian correctional officers are two examples. Of the 104,000 non-sworn civilian personnel over one-half (61,290) are in jail related positions. In other words, about 2 of every 5 sheriff department employees works in jail-related positions (Reaves, and Hickman, 2001).Like the other components of the criminal justice system, corrections is predominately a male occupation. Of the almost 14,000 officers in the Federal Bureau of Prisons 86.9 percent of the correctional officers are male and 13. 1 percent are female. When these officers are classified by ethnicity, whites account for 60.8 percent, blacks account for 24.5 percent, and Hispanics account for 12.1 percent (Reaves and Hart, 2001). According to the American Correctional Association's Directory (2001), of the 19 states which provide information on this subject, females accounted for only 27 percent of all correctional officers.

TABLE 1.5
CHARACTERISTICS OF AMERICAN PRISONS
2000

ALL FACILITIES	1,208
INMATE GENDER	
male	1,017
female	98
both	93
FUNCTION	
holding general adult population	1,081
boot camp	84
reception, diagnosis, or classification	173
medical treatment or hospitalization	142
alcohol and/or drug treatment	200
holding youthful offenders	36
work release/pre-release	107
holding persons returned to custody	58
other	317
AVERAGE DAILY POPULATION	
fewer than 100	53
100-249	173
250-749	327
750-1,499	417
1,500-2,499	174
2,500 or more	64

Source: Bureau of Justice Statistics. (2003). *Census of State and Federal Correctional Facilities, 2002.* Washington, D.C.: U.S. Department of Justice.

In Texas, of the more than 24,000 officers 37.5 percent are female; in California, of the nearly 21,000 officers almost 19 percent are female. Twenty eight percent of the correctional officers in Texas and 14 percent of the correctional officers in California are black. Nineteen percent of the officers in Texas and over 29 percent of the officers in California are Hispanic.

The mission statement of the Texas Department of Criminal Justice - Institutional Division "is to provide safe and appropriate confinement, supervision, rehabilitation and reintegration of adult felons, and to effectively manage or administer correctional facilities based on constitutional and statutory standards" (Texas Department of Criminal Justice, n.d.). In Arkansas, a Correctional Officer I is responsible for maintaining security and overseeing the work of inmates in a correctional facility. Frequent shift-work and exposure to danger from inmates is required as is frequent 24 hour emergency on-call duty. The starting salary is $20,000 annually. In Florida correctional officers "are responsible for the supervision, care, custody, control, and physical restraint, when necessary, of inmates in a correctional institution or facility. Correctional Officers are assigned to any one of several security posts on any of the established shifts" (Florida Department of Corrections, n.d.). Some of the duties and responsibilities of a Correctional Officer I (COI) include: supervising inmates in housing units; instructing inmates in housekeeping and sanitation; supervising the issuance of clothing and other personal effects to inmates; make periodic patrols of quarters and work areas; conduct regular and irregular counts of inmates; maintain control and discipline to include the use of physical restraint as well as deterring the introduction of contraband into the institution (Florida Department of Corrections, n.d., p. 1). According to the Florida Department of Corrections other duties include: checking inmates for contraband, maintaining periodic patrols to ensure the security band integrity of the institution; to monitor, supervise and screen inmate visitor traffic and to observe traffic in and around the compound. Correctional Officers also maintain records of equipment, demonstrate proficiency in the use and care of firearms, restraint equipment, communication and other electronic equipment as well as instruct inmates in the proper care and use of institutional equipment. The Florida Department of Corrections website also provides a description of the various posts a correctional officer might work. For example, the Dormitory Post requires the constant walking and patrolling of an area, in and out of buildings. There is also continuous inmate contact including searches of inmates and property. The continuous use of keys, preparing and maintaining logs, and other reports is required. The Control Room Post requires the constant use of the telephone, radio, public address system, electronic door switches as well as computer keyboard and typewriter. This website provides detailed explanations of each post along with the shift schedule and minimal qualifications. Starting salary for a trainee officer is more than $25,000 annually. With duties and responsibilities similar to that of a state correctional officer the starting salary for a correctional officer with the Federal Bureau of Prisons in 2002 was more than $30,000.

Other Correctional Staff

It should be noted that prisons are not just wardens, correctional officers, and inmates. Modern correctional facilities emulate a modern civilian community, in which a variety of occupational categories are required to keep the community functioning. *Counselors and psychologists* help diagnose, evaluate, and treat offenders. *Medical personnel* provide required services. *Administrative personnel* are involved in the extensive record keeping required. *Educational personnel* provided academic and technical/vocational training as needed. This panoply of personnel is detailed in Table 1.6.

TABLE 1.6
CORRECTIONAL EMPLOYEES 2000

	Federal	State	Private
Administration	1,743	8,953	1,448
Custody/Security	12,376	243,352	14,589
Clerical/main't/food	1,670	48,463	2,599
Education	832	11,763	1,093
Professional/Tech	11,686	41,499	2,997
Other	4,393	18,946	1,631

Source: Bureau of Justice Statistics. (2001). *Census of State and Federal Correctional Facilities, 2000.* Washington, D.C.: U.S. Department of Justice.

Summary

Prisons in America have evolved over the years in response to the needs of society. As society moved from notions of retaliation and punishment, to rehabilitation, and then to justice, prisons too were forced to change. As their functions have changed, so have the roles of those who provide security within their walls. The job of the correctional officer has expended from mere custody to a complex multi-faceted occupation. The correctional officer corps has evolved into a diverse group of professionals. As we have seen, the modern American correctional system has grown into a complex, professional industry, employing hundreds of thousands of individuals responsible for supervising over two million inmates.

2

SELECTION AND TRAINING

Given the stresses and dangers of prison work, one might wonder why and how people become correctional officers. According to Josi & Sechrest (1998: 3) "corrections has been viewed as an occupational field, not a profession." Unlike many other actors in the criminal justice system, correctional officers have had an image problem. As the least visible and least understood actor in the system, it is difficult for those in the field of corrections to provide an accurate view of their professional world. Yet correctional organizations are doing a better job today in disseminating information about the field of corrections than in the past. The Federal Bureau of Prisons, along with many state and local correctional departments, maintain internet sites which provide vast amounts of information about these organizations. There are even internet sites which provide links to all state correctional organizations. These internet sites can provide information about employment, training, salaries, duties of correctional officers, departmental histories, as well as a wealth of information on inmates.

As noted earlier, until the 1970s and the 1980s corrections was seen merely as an occupational field, not as a professional activity. Lombardo (1989), in his study of correctional officers in New York, found that many of those involved in his research had previously held factory or construction jobs. For these individuals job security was the primary reason for becoming a correctional officer. One officer commented "I was getting more money on my other job in 1968, but I was only working six to nine months a year. The guard's job only paid $5,600 when I started, but you got a check every month" (Lombardo, 1989: 28). Another officer said "I had two uncles and a cousin who worked (at Auburn Prison). They came home clean, not dirty. They said you didn't really work. I thought it was easier to work there than in the print shop, so I got in" (Lombardo, 1989: 29). When asked the question "*how did you come to be a correctional officer?*" the majority of those in Lombardo's study replied that their major motivation was either for job security or for pay and benefits. In Kauffman's study of Massachusetts' recruits, "slightly more than half (53 percent) of the forty recruits cited economic considerations as their only or primary reason for becoming prison officers" (1998: 170). A steady pay check was the primary economic factor for many who became correctional officers.

As Kauffman so aptly states, "corrections is not a high-profile career, one that readily comes to mind to the average job seeker" (1988: 169). Many found out about correctional openings by word of mouth from other family members. Three-fourths of the recruits in Kauffman's study and two-thirds of the officers in Lombardo's study had relatives employed in corrections.

Early History of Correctional Officers

The story of punishing wrong-doers is as old as the story of humanity. Although the methods of determining guilt and the methods of sanctioning those found guilty have changed over time, the basic premise has not. Whether possessed by the devil or acting of their own free will, individuals who violated the norms of a given society or social structure were required to pay for those transgressions. Corporal punishment, death, or banishment from the group were early common practices. (For an in-depth examination of punishment see Harry Elmer Barnes' (1972) *The Story of Punishment: A Record of Man's Inhumanity to Man* or George Ives' (1970) *A History of Penal Methods: Criminals, Witches, Lunatics.*) The rise of nation states in the middle ages brought about a shift in the purpose of punishment. As mentioned earlier, crimes and punishment were seen as private wrongs, and revenge was seen as the main purpose of punishment. An "eye for an eye," - revenge and retribution - were the justification for punishment. By the twelfth century England had developed a rudimentary criminal justice system. Now crimes were considered offenses against the king and the king could, therefore, require punishment. The sheriff was the king's representative in the local shire (county). The sheriff would detain a wrongdoer in the local gaol (jail) until the circuit judge could hear a case. Still, at this time, incarceration was not a method of carrying out the sentence of the court. Such corporal punishments as flogging, mutilation, and branding were predominate methods used in the middle ages. Confinement was reserved for political prisoners or debtors. The dungeons in the Tower of London held political prisoners of the crown or the commonwealth and the Fleet Street Prison was used primarily to hold debtors until debts could be paid off. "It thus became known as a debtors' prison" (Brown, 1996: 4). Torture, gaols, dungeons, towers, debtors' prisons, workhouses, asylums, hulks, transportation and prisons were all forms used by governments to imprison and punish wrongdoers. But by the Eighteenth Century reform movements were underway to improve the way criminals were treated.

In the United States, the Philadelphia Society for Alleviating the Miseries of the Public Prisons was one of the first groups to advocate changes in how prisoners were treated. Organized in the 1780s, this group was instrumental in getting the Pennsylvania criminal code modified and advocated the use of prisons (Heffernan, 1985). By the second decade of the nineteenth century the penitentiary system was the predominate mode of incarceration for convicted offenders.

The individuals who ran the prison systems and those who worked for prison systems obtained their jobs just like all other government employees of the time - through political appointment. The political patronage system was the dominate force in American politics through much of our history. The civil service system began in the federal government in the late 1800s, but it would take another 30 to 50 years before civil service systems were implemented by state and local governments.

During the early 1900s correctional officers were inadequately trained, underpaid, and overworked. Twelve hour shifts were the norm with many officers working up to sixteen hours a day, six days a week. According to an early twentieth century report prisons were "the dumping grounds for the inefficient and the unfit relatives and political hangers-on of the professional politicians ...." (Josi & Sechrest, 1998: 4). They were described as being cold, sadistic, and punitive.

Jacobs (1977) in his study of Illinois' Stateville Prison reported that, on average, in 1935 there were 225 officers for 3,400 inmates; a 1:15 ratio. By the 1970s the ratio was 1:3.75, or 400 officers for 1,500 inmates. During the early twentieth century in Illinois, many officers were political appointees, untrained with no job security. A 1928 commission report said "guards were politically appointed, untrained for their work ..... with no assurance of tenure or pension, underpaid, many physically unfit for crises, inexperienced in prison conditions....." (Jacobs, 1977: 21). A political change of governor resulted in large scale job turnover in the correctional system as it was for every other political appointment. This persisted until the 1970s. One of the recommendations of the President's Task Force on Corrections was "the warden and all other employees of correctional institutions should be appointed through the competitive selection process of a merit system" (1967: 209). By the 1970s the movement to professionalize administrators and officers was well underway nationwide.

Three developments in the 1970s brought substantial changes to the position of correctional officer. Jacobs (1977) identified these developments as: the introduction of reform administrators; the advent of public employee unionism; and the increased racial and gender integration of correctional officers. Jacobs (1977) and Lombardo (1989), in their studies of Stateville in Illinois and Auburn in New York, indicate that prior to this time correctional officers were predominately white males. Irwin (1980) characterized the typical correctional officer as a white male from a small town or rural area with a minimal amount of education and a history of unemployment. Many chose this vocation later in life with a variety of employment backgrounds.

Prior to civil service and the professionalization of officers and administrators in Illinois, Jacobs (1977) reported that all wardens in the state had come up through the ranks and none had a college education. By 1974, no warden had started as an officer, and six of the eight had masters degrees.

Becoming a Correctional Officer

As previously reported, the main qualification for a job in corrections was political patronage. This could be more prevalent in some states than others. Job security was nonexistent as personnel changed with each political election. Pay was low, minimum qualifications varied, and work conditions were harsh. The President's Commission on Law enforcement and Administration of Justice Task Force Report: Corrections (1967) reported "the recruitment problems of corrections are aggravated by low salaries, long working hours, lack of effective contacts with colleges and universities, and other specific handicaps (1967: 93).

The average annual salary for a corrections officer in 1967 was between \$3,000 - \$4,000. Officers were described for the most part as "undereducated, untrained, and unversed in the goals of corrections (1967: 95). The Commission complained that in "many correctional systems, employment policies do not encourage people of ability, and standards for recruitment and promotion are not adequate" (1967: 94).

There are no, as yet, national qualification standards for correctional officers. Qualifications vary by state and local agency based upon the needs of a given agency. For example, to qualify at the GS - 5 level in the Federal Bureau of Prisons a person must have a full 4 year course of study in any field leading to a bachelor's degree from an accredited school or the possession of a bachelor's degree; or the equivalent of at least 3 years of full time experience in correctional related activities; or a combination of undergraduate education and general experience equivalent to 3 years of full time experience. As of January 2002 the basic starting annual salary was more than \$30,000. To qualify as a GS - 6 a person must have at least 9 semester hours of graduate study from an accredited school in criminal justice or a related field, or one year of full time specialized experience performing corrections related duties. The starting annual salary at this level is over \$32,000 (BOP. n.d.).

The basic qualifications for a correctional officer in Texas are: 1) be a U.S. citizen or authorized alien, 2) be at least 18 years old, 3) possess a high school diploma or GED, and 4) must pass the TDCJ pre-employment test and the TDCJ drug test and basically can not be convicted of a crime. The starting salary for a Texas CO is more than \$20,000 a year (TDCJ, n.d.).

In Florida, in order to become a correctional officer you must; be a U.S. citizen, at least 19 years old, be a high school graduate, not convicted of any felony or of a misdemeanor involving perjury or a false statement, nor have received a dishonorable discharge from any of the armed forces. An applicant has to pass a physical examination, have good moral character, and pass the basic recruit training course. The starting annual salary for a trainee officer is over $25,000 (FDOC, n.d.).

To be eligible to take the CO examination in California you must; have no felony convictions, be a U.S. resident or permanent resident alien, be a high school graduate or possess a GED, and have a history of law abiding behavior. Starting salary for a California CO is over $33,000 annually (CDC, n.d.). To qualify as a CO 1 in Alabama's corrections department you must be; a U.S. citizen, at least 20 years of age at time of appointment, be in good health and physically fit, possess a high school diploma or GED equivalent with no felony convictions or domestic violence convictions of any kind. If a prior a member of the armed forces the applicant must have been honorably discharged. The starting salary is over $23,000 annually.

While there are no national standards for correctional officers the minimal qualifications are rather consistent across the country. The minimum age can range from eighteen to twenty - one. A high school diploma or GED is the minimal educational requirement. For the Federal Bureau of Prisons educational requirements can vary from a bachelor's degree to a combination of college and work experience. Some states require a valid driver license. For states which require correctional officers to handle firearms an individual can not be convicted of a felony or have a domestic violence conviction. Starting salaries range from the lower the twenties to the lower thirty thousands of dollars.

The selection process can include taking a state standardized written examination, a physical examination, drug testing, oral interviews and psychological evaluations. Individuals who meet the minimum qualifications for a correctional officer in Ohio will go through the correctional officer assessment which includes: Correctional Officers Video test, physical agility test (including 3/4 mile run, lifting and moving 50 pound locker, search and shakedown of a bunk,

Adult Measurement of Essential Skill (AMES) test, an interview, a background investigation, and a drug test (ODRC, n.d.). North Carolina explains that the COVT (correctional officer video test) is a situational judgment test. Ergometrics & Applied Personnel Research Inc. of Edmonds, Washington, provides a COVT which consists of 83 real - life job scenarios presented on video. Applicants watch each scenario and make a judgment about how to respond using multiple choice answers (Ergometrics' COVT, n.d.). This test is designed to test inmate, co-worker and supervisor relation skills. According to the manufacturer, "this test is an efficient and cost effective way to identify applicants early in the screening process who have a high likelihood of becoming outstanding officers" (Ergometrics' COVT, n.d.: 2) (underline original) North Carolina also requires psychological and drug testing along with a complete physical examination (NCDC, n.d.).

Below is the selection process and timetable for prospective California Correctional Officers. California's Department of Corrections maintains a detailed web site for all aspects of the correctional system (see www.cdc.state.ca.us). While each state's selection process varies, California's selection process is highlighted because of the detailed information provide on it's internet site.

Selection Process

1. Submit Application: Scoring Category Worksheet (SCW). Candidates are scored based upon work habits, education and self-improvement efforts, and law abiding behavior. This work sheet determines if an individual meets the minimum requirements to continue the selection process. Individuals who pass this stage will be scheduled for the written examination.

2. Within 7 Days CO applicants are scheduled for CO written examination and the Peace Officer Psychological Examination (POPE): Examinations are given periodically at selected locations through the state. These are pass/fail tests.

Sample tests are available on-line.

3. Candidates take the Written Correctional Officer Examination, Written Psychological Examination, provided a Personal History Statement form (PHS), and are given a date to participate in the physical abilities test (PAT): The written examination is designed to evaluate skills in grammar, spelling, punctuation, reading comprehension and basic mathematics. At this stage the psychological examination is a written examination. Written examination are pass/ fail.

4. Candidates submit the PHS, and undergo a Vision Test, Risk Assessment, PAT, and Fingerprinting: The vision test determines distant and color vision. To pass, visual acuity must be 20/60 in each eye correctable to 20/20 with glasses. Color vision must be adequate. Before taking the PAT an individual will undergo a risk assessment which includes height and weight measurement, blood pressure check, coronary risk assessment, and a review of current health status. Passing the risk assessment allows an individual to participate in the PAT. The physical abilities test consists of five physically demanding tests designed to evaluate overall fitness to perform specific functions of a correctional officer. These tests measure overall endurance, grip strength, trunk strength, dynamic arm endurance, and dynamic leg endurance. The physical abilities test measures physical activities that a correctional officer could likely engage in during his or her career. This test includes:

4.a Dynamic Arm Test - This test requires the test taker to sit on the floor behind a stationary bike, in a straddle position. Test takers use hands and arms to pedal a bicycle ergometer with 2.5 kps of resistance. The test taker must complete 45 revolutions in one minute. The test predicts a person's ability to carry a stretcher containing a 185 pound person 1/8 of a mile with the assistance of another person and another 1/8 of a mile with the assistance of 3 other people.

4.b Dynamic Leg Test - This test requires the test taker to pedal a stationary bike and complete 70 revolutions in a minute utilizing 3.0 kps of resistance on the ergometer. This test simulates a person's ability to sprint 100 yards in less than 20 seconds.

4.c Pedal Test- This is a three minute test on a stationary bicycle ergometer. The first minute is for warm up and the last two minutes are at a pre-determined pace. The amount of resistance is based upon a person's weight. This test simulates a person's ability to run in full uniform 500 yards in less than two minutes.

4.d Trunk Strength Test-This exercise requires the test taker to exert a maximal force against a cable tensiometer (a harness worn across the shoulders, chest and back, connected to cables). It measures flexibility and extension of the upper body. The test simulates running 500 yards and then dragging an unconscious person weighing 165 pounds 20 feet in 20 seconds or less.

4.f Grip Strength Test -This is a test of the dominant hand using a hand grip dynamometer. The test measures the same requirements as does the dynamic arm test. A person is given 3 opportunities to pass the PAT in 6 months. A passing score is valid for one year. The California Department of Correction's web site offers exercise suggestions which can help prepare a person to take the PAT.

5. Background Investigation- A thorough background investigation is conducted. Investigators will verify information provided during the selection process. Family, friends, acquaintances, landlords, school officials, supervisors and coworkers will be contacted. Criminal history checks will be conducted at the local, state and federal level as well as checks with the department of motor vehicles and other governmental agencies as needed. Checks are made to verify information and evaluate a person's character.

6. State Personnel Board (SPB) will schedule a personal interview with a psychologist.

7. The Pre-Employment Medical Examination (PEM) can consist urinalysis, complete blood count, blood chemistry panel, a general physical examination and other tests if needed.

After passing the selection process a person is ranked by final score. Assignment to one of the 33 facilities is based upon departmental need. As assignments become available a candidate is notified and has 7 to 10 days to accept or reject the assignment. After accepting the assignment the candidate will attend the next sixteen week Basic Correctional Officers Academy (BOCA). The average time frame from application to completion of Selection Process takes between 4 to 10 months. It can be a rather slow process, but it is necessary for recruiting quality personnel.

Training

For the greater part of the history of corrections the training of correctional officers was a rather haphazard endeavor. Most training was on the job. There were no formal training academies until the middle of the twentieth century. The President's Commission on Law enforcement and Administration of Justice Task Force Report: Corrections (1967) reported "perhaps the most striking finding was the more than half of the responding agencies have no organized training programs at all" (1967: 100). Lombardo (1989) reported that prior to the creation of the New York State Correctional Services Training Academy in 1972, New York State correctional officers were trained on the job. According to Lombardo (1989:40) "inmates trained officers." As one officer at Auburn reported "An inmate broke me in ....Really! He told me to stand back and he showed me how and where to frisk" (Lombardo, 1989:40). Many of the officers interviewed by Lombardo "who entered prison service prior to 1972, reported that they were simply issued a badge, a club and a hat, shown the yard and told to go to work" (Lombardo 1989:35).

Lombardo (1989) reported that with the creation of the New York State Correctional Services Training Academy in 1972, new correctional officers received 13 weeks of training, 10 weeks of classroom training, and 3 weeks of training on the job. In North Carolina, in 1974, the state Criminal Justice Academy was founded and began training correctional staff. That same year Missouri established a formal training program for correctional officers. By the 1970s state-operated basic training academies became the preferred method for training new correctional officers. Just as in the selection process the training process varies from state to state. North Carolina's Correctional Officer Basic Training Program is a four week, 160 hour program; the Illinois Department of Corrections and the Oklahoma Department of Corrections requires all new correctional officers to complete a six week basic academy, while Mississippi's academy is seven weeks long. Alabama's basic correctional officer academy is ten weeks, while California's academy is sixteen weeks long.

California's Basic Correctional Officer Academy is detailed in the following paragraphs. California is again highlighted as a result of their detailed internet website (cdc.state.ca.us. n.d).

Correctional Officers must complete a sixteen-week, formal, comprehensive training program at the Basic Correctional Officer Academy (BCOA), located in Galt, a suburb south of Sacramento. Cadets will attend classes five days a week and must pass all tests in order to graduate from the BCOA. The training program seeks to instill the skills and experience needed to function in a prison setting and to build *esprit de corps* among the cadets. This is done using a combination of academic instruction, physical fitness training, use of force awareness, group interaction, and communication skills.

The curriculum consists of 640 hours of training. Correctional officer cadets begin each day with a nutritious breakfast, then attend various academic courses, or motor skills training that includes: Peace Officer Standards and Training Courses (POST), firearms training, chemical agents, impact weapons training, and arrest and control techniques. Classroom instruction covers several other subjects related to the specific functions of a correctional peace officer such as laws of arrest, constitutional rights, rules and concepts of evidence, rights of the confined, effects/use of force, disciplinary process, restraint devices, cell and person searches, transportation, prison gangs, and crime victims.

Correctional officer cadets receive continuous reinforcement with emphasis being placed on integrity, maturity, professional conduct, written and verbal communication skills, interaction, professionalism, and competency-based evaluations to demonstrate proficiency in these areas.

Cadets now have the choice to either live on or off site during the duration of the Academy. Specifics on cadet orientation can be found in the Cadet Handbook received by a new CO once an assignment is accepted. Cadets report to their assigned institutions on the first Monday following graduation.

Once the cadet completes the 16-week training and graduates from the academy, he or she must then complete a two-year apprenticeship program. During this two-year period, the new CO receives on-the-job training enhanced with certain required courses taught at the institution. As an apprentice, the new CO is given a wide variety of assignments and is expected to meet specified work standards to increase his/her ability to function effectively in a prison setting. In addition to the BCOA, the Apprenticeship Program and an orientation program for new employees, all COs receive monthly training on an on-going basis at their respective institutions.

For a new cadet at the Oklahoma Correctional Officer Pre-Service Academy at the Gene Stipe Correctional Training Academy located on the campus of Eastern Oklahoma State College in Wilburton, classes begin at 7:15 a.m. and end at 6:45 p.m. Monday through Thursday. Tests are scheduled weekly. Week One consists of classes detailing orientation to the academy; an overview of the Department of Corrections and the criminal justice system; classes on physical conditioning and wellness; sexual harassment; defensive driving, and report writing. Training in Week Two includes classes on effective communication; workplace violence; an overview of legal aspects; firearms training; environmental security procedures, and physical training. Week Three continues with more classes on environmental security procedures; more physical conditioning and classes on blood - borne pathogens. Week Four begins with classes on a healthier work environment; creating a positive public image; conflict resolution, practical reasoning; use of force; use of restraints; first aid and CPR; behavioral recognition and more physical conditioning. Week Five is devoted entirely to self defense training. The final week of classes focuses on disciplinary procedures; riot prevention and control; hostage first responder; hostage situations, and still more physical conditioning. For an in-depth examination of Oklahoma's Pre - Service Training Academy visit their web site (www.doc.state.ok.us/training/cotrain.htm).

In-Service Training

Training does not stop once a new officer leaves the academy. Many states provide orientation training at each facility. For example, the Corrections Training Academy of the Ohio Department of Rehabilitation and Correction's "offers many diverse courses to provide for the needs of the employees and prepare qualified instructors to cascade training to all institutions and office sites" (ODRC, n.d.: 2). The curriculum includes areas of instructional development, instructor training, as well as individual and professional development. Training is conducted at the Training Academy and at regional sites throughout the state.

Specialized training curricula are also offered at the Training Academy. Training can range from executive leadership courses to advanced medical courses to critical incident management. Courses are also available for specialized teams such as hostage negotiations, special tactics and response, riflemen training, and stress debriefing teams.

The National Institute of Corrections (NIC), part of the Bureau of Prisons within the U. S. Department of Justice, provides training, technical assistance, information services, and policy/ program development for federal, state and local corrections agencies. The NIC provides management and specialty training for practitioners working in state and local agencies through a variety of training delivery systems. Practitioners can participate in classroom-based training programs conducted at the NIC facility in Longmont, Colorado or at other sites throughout the country. Practitioners can view Satellite and Internet broadcasts of video conferences or participate in distance learning programs, or the NIC can provide training by conducting workshops at professional correctional conferences (National Institute of Corrections n.d.). Camp's (2003) complete state-by state description can be found in Table 2.1.

County and Local Jails

Qualifications and employment opportunities for correctional officers vary greatly among the more than 3,000 sheriff departments and 12,000 police departments in the United States. Correctional officers at the county level can be commissioned law enforcement officers, who have completed the basic law enforcement training as stipulated by the state, or non-sworn officers who have completed the proscribed basic jailers training academy.

TABLE 2.1
CORRECTIONAL OFFICER TRAINING
& PROBATIONARY PERIODS 2002

State	Probation (months)	Pre-Service (hrs)	In-Service (hrs)	State	Probation (months)	Pre-Service (hrs)	In-Service (hrs)
Alabama	6	480	40	Nebraska	6	200	40
Alaska	13	240	40	Nevada	12	260	24
Arizona	12	280	40	New Hampshire	12	320	40
Arkansas	12	240	40	New Jersey	16	560	16
California	12	640	40	New Mexico	12	280	40
Colorado	12	152	40	New York	12	440	40
Connecticut	9	210	40	North Carolina	12	160	40
Delaware	12	320	22	North Dakota	6	160	43
D.C.	12	240	40	Ohio	12	280	40
Florida	12	530	40	Oklahoma	12	344	40
Georgia		184	24	Oregon	12	280	40
Idaho	12	200	40	Pennsylvania	12	200	40
Illinois	4.5	240	40	Rhode Island	6	360	16
Indiana		160	40	South Carolina	12	240	40
Iowa	6	180	40	South Dakota	6	200	40
Kansas	12	200	80	Tennessee	6	360	40
Kentucky	8	240	40	Texas		316	40
Louisiana	6	120	40	Utah	18	499	40
Maine	6	80	16	Vermont	6		
Maryland	12	240	18	Virginia	12	400	40
Massachusetts	9	320	40	Washington	12	200	40
Michigan	12	640	40	West Virginia		240	40
Minnesota	6	240	40	Wisconsin	7.8	280	8
Mississippi	12	280	40	Wyoming	12	120	40
Missouri		240	40	Federal	12	200	40
Montana		180	40	Average	10.3	280	37

Just as the qualifications and training requirements vary from state to state, qualifications and training for jail security staff also varies by state and can vary within a state. State legislatures outline in state statutes or state administrative codes the academic requirements for certification of a commissioned peace officer or the certification of a jailer. In Wisconsin, for example, some sheriff's departments utilize commissioned deputy sheriffs to work in the jails. The qualifications and training for this position are the same as for deputies engaged in law enforcement activities. Dane County Sheriff's Department starts all deputies in the jail. A deputy can expect to spend up to five years working in the jail before being assigned to the road. New deputies first attended the ten week basic law enforcement academy, the three week basic state jail officer school, and the Sheriff's Office eight week in-house Jail Training Program before beginning work. The ten week, 400 hour, basic law enforcement academy is standard through the state of Wisconsin. All law enforcement officers in the state must attend a state sanctioned regional law enforcement academy. The same applies to the three week basic jail officer school. Counties which employ civilian jailers are required to send all new jailers to a basic jail officer school. Dane County also employs civilian jail clerks to relieve deputies from many mundane administrative tasks. According to the Department's web site "This position will handle transactions with other employees or the public in matters requiring detailed knowledge of laws, rules, procedures, policies, precedents and activities; perform booking intake, bail/release, records update and other related duties as assigned" (Dane County Sheriff's Department, n.d.: 1). Qualifications for this position include a high school diploma and at least two years of clerical experience. Some of the abilities required for this position are the ability to deal effectively with a heavy workload; the ability to handle large sums of money for inmate cash and bail; the ability to perform data entry and the *ability to deal with difficult and angry people* (italics added).

The Bucks County, Pennsylvania, Department of Corrections employs over 300 people in a variety of jobs. Correctional officers with this organization receive 176 hours of classroom instruction and on-the-job training. Successful candidates with this organization must be 18 years old, possess a high school diploma or GED, have a valid driver's license and complete the Department of Corrections Basic Training Class.

The New York City Department of Corrections employs over 10,000 uniformed staff and 1,500 civilian staff to monitor a daily population which averages between 14,000 - 19,000 inmates. The New York City Department of Corrections boasts a larger daily inmate population "than the entire prison system in any of 35 states" (Department Overview, n.d.: 1). Applicants go through a grueling selection process and successful applicants complete a 15 week training academy before assignment to one of the 10 facilities on Rikers Island, located in the East River, or to one of the borough jails.

Most city jails are managed by that city's police department, not a separate correctional department. Over half of all police departments in this country employ 10 or fewer full-time officers. Ninety percent of all departments have fewer than 50 officers (Reaves and Goldberg, 1998). America is a country of small police departments, many of which do not hold prisoners for any length of time. These departments must rely up the local sheriff's department to provide jail facilities. Almost two-thirds of the 3,000+ sheriffs' departments have fewer than 25 full-time, sworn officers. Nonetheless, nationwide, about 30 percent of all sworn deputies work in jail operations. Jail operations are a major function of a sheriff's department along with patrol, investigation, and court operations.

A growing field in corrections is the privatization of security services. Governments are contracting out to private industry the running of correctional facilities, including the security force. During the 1980s, in an effort to reduce overcrowding and lower costs, public correctional systems began exploring the idea of privatizing corrections. Two of the largest private correctional services in this country are Correctional Service Corporation (CSC) and Corrections Corporation of America (CCA). CSC operates 13 adult facilities and 33 juvenile facilities in 18 states (CSC, 2001). CCA operates 60 facilities in 21 states (CCA, n.d.). CCA provides services for federal, state and local governments. The qualifications to become a private correctional officer are similar to the qualification for becoming a state correctional officer. A correctional officer for CCA must have a high school diploma or GED, a valid driver's license, and complete the pre- service correctional officer training and, where applicable, be a non-commissioned security officer licensed by the state of employment. Higher ranking positions are available based upon higher educational levels or criminal justice-related work experience (CCA, n.d.).

Turnover

Attracting quality candidates into the correctional officers corps is all for naught if prisons are unable to retain their services. However, many correctional systems have a difficult time with this task. This is not too surprising, considering the daunting, difficult, and sometimes dangerous conditions in which they work. COs are, after all, locked in correctional facilities like the inmates during their shifts.

Losing correctional officers to other careers is problematic for correctional facilities at many levels. First, correctional agencies spend a great deal of time, effort, and money training applicants to be correctional officers. The longer an officer stays with the department, the more beneficial the cost/benefit ratio that accrues to the department. Secondly, much of a correctional officer's job is learned through experience with inmates. This knowledge many times can only be

42

TABLE 2.2
CORRECTIONAL OFFICER TURNOVER RATES 2001

State	Total Officers	Turnover Rate (%)	State	Total Officers	Turnover Rate (%)
Alabama	264	11.9	Nebraska	199	26
Alaska	55		Nevada	173	13.6
Arizona	1,008	21.6	New Hampshire	94	18
Arkansas	811	39	New Jersey	331	6
California	1,167	17	New Mexico	112	10.6
Colorado			New York	688	3.5
Connecticut	131	3	North Carolina	2,348	19.8
Delaware	278	13	North Dakota	31	15
D.C.	264	20	Ohio	605	8.1
Florida	1,833	20	Oklahoma	257	11.2
Georgia	1,907		Oregon	135	8.7
Idaho	159	23.2	Pennsylvania	464	5.3
Illinois	692	6.7	Rhode Island	24	3
Indiana	1,033	24.1	South Carolina	1,186	29.8
Iowa	132	7	South Dakota	74	25.3
Kansas	414	25.2	Tennessee	639	28.1
Kentucky	332	28	Texas	5,459	23
Louisiana	1,383	33	Utah	51	9
Maine		17	Vermont	44	10
Maryland	899	13.6	Virginia	857	13.3
Massachusetts	36		Washington	270	10.7
Michigan	366	3.9	West Virginia		12
Minnesota	160	10.1	Wisconsin	455	
Mississippi	525	22.4	Wyoming	126	36.7
Missouri	4519	34	Federal	816	5.6
Montana		20	Average	33,806	16.6

Source: Camp, C. (2003). *The Corrections Yearbook 2002.* Middleton, CT: Criminal Justice Institute, Inc.

learned through experience. COs must spend months, if not years, learning "the inmate". High turnover rates therefore ensure that officers may lack the knowledge necessary to run the prison both effectively and safely. The data detailing turnover rates of CO's is presented in Table 2.2. Nationwide, in 2001, the average turnover rate for correctional officers was 16.6%. Note that the state with the highest turnover rate was Arkansas (39%), while the lowest turnover rate occurred in Rhode Island and Connecticut (3%) (Camp, 2003).

Summary

Becoming a correctional officer is far more difficult today than in the past. Rather than merely a political patronage appointment, the correctional officer today must go through a rigorous selection and training process. While there are no nation-wide standards, training and educational levels for correctional officers have increased in both the state and federal systems, with the federal system generally employing better educated officers.

Jails too employ correctional officers, and they are in many ways similar to their prison counterparts. One important difference is that jail deputies who perform the correctional officer role are generally trained as law enforcement officers first, and correctional experts second. Thus, jails have also begun to employ COs trained specifically for jail work.

Regardless of employer, all COs face daunting challenges in providing prison security. These difficulties many times force officers to leave the field, thus resulting in high turnover rates and the resulting employment of newer, less experienced, replacements. Thus while recruiting higher qualified correctional officers than in the past, a goal for the future of corrections should be to find a way to retain these trained and experienced individuals.

3

CHARACTERISTICS OF CORRECTIONAL OFFICERS

Correctional officers share many characteristics. However, unlike times past, one would now be mistaken to stereotype the average correctional officer as a mid-to-late twenties, married, white male, with a high school diploma from a rural area. According to May (1981: 21) "unlike the picture of the Hollywood guard, his real life counterpart does not lend himself to a capsule portrait. There is no national model. There is none even within a single state or, for that matter, within different prisons under the jurisdiction of the same department." May further states (1981: 21), "the inability to generalize about the contemporary correctional officer even is apparent inside one single institution. Attitudes, behavior, enforcement of regulations differ markedly from shift to shift."

There is no national model for the average correctional officer. There is no national data bank maintained about correctional officers. The American Correctional Association's (ACA) annual directory and reports from the Bureau of Justice Statistics provide some aggregate data about correctional officers nationwide, including the number of officers employed by each state as well as officers employed by county correctional facilities. All state departments of corrections maintain official web sites. Vast amounts of information are provided about institutions, inmates, and goods and services provided, but there is little information available about correctional officers.

Florida's Department of Corrections' 2001-2002 Annual Report (Annual Report, 2002) reports that there are 14,800 correctional officers employed by the department. Almost 70 percent are classified as correctional officers, another 29 percent are sergeants, lieutenants, or captains, with the remaining 1.5 percent being higher-ranking officers. Kansas' 2002 corrections briefing report indicates that the average age of the uniformed staff is 40.9 years, 80.7 percent of which are male and 87.7 percent are white. Correctional Officers I (the lowest ranking officer) account for 35 percent of all staff and over half of all uniformed staff. About a quarter of all CO I's had less than three years work experience with the department (Kansas 2002 Corrections Briefing Report, 2002).

Most detailed information about correctional officers comes from researchers examining one system or one facility, or by conducting surveys with one or several systems, or surveys of several facilities within a system, or the survey of officers working in one facility. Demographic information about correctional officers is just one of the many measures or variables researchers collect and examine. While perhaps not the main focus of a research project, the demographic characteristics provides a snapshot of officers who were working at a particular facility or within a given system at the time of the study. The Federal Bureau of Prisons provides ongoing information about that system and allows researchers access to correctional officers.

Federal Correctional Officers

A brief review of several demographic characteristics of correctional officers employed by the Federal Bureau of Prisons in 2002. On January 1 of that year there over 217,570 COs employed in the United States. Of these officers,

76.7% were male and 23% were female. Racially and ethnically, most officers were white (69.7%) and 30% minority. The distribution of minority COs was 21.7% black, 6.3% Hispanic, 1.3% Native American, .07% Asian Pacific, and 1.2% were categorized as "other" (Camp and Camp, 2003). By the beginning of the 21st Century the racial and sexual composition of officers in the federal system was vastly different than the stereotypical white male of earlier eras.

In examining the age distribution, almost three of every five BOP correctional officers (57.3 %) were between 30 and 40 years of age, while about 20 percent were under thirty and about 24 percent were over 40 years of age. This age distribution is reflective of the growth of the BOP during the late 1980s and the early 1990s, as the federal prison population more than doubled during this time. Increases in the prison population corresponded with hiring more correctional officers. This is indicative of the fact that by the end of 1999, almost half (48.8%) of males and 40.4 percent of female correctional officers had been with the BOP between 5 and 14 years, putting their original employment dates between 1985 and 1995. Since 1995, the BOP has continued to grow, and over half of all correctional officers (53% of males and 55% of females) had fewer than 5 years on the job. Stiffer drug laws and mandatory sentencing account for the tremendous growth of inmates in the Federal Bureau of Prisons, quadrupling their numbers between 1985 and 2001. As of October 1, 2001, well over half (55%) of the 160,000+ federal inmates were serving time for drug offenses and almost four of every ten inmates were serving sentences ranging from 10 years to life (Federal Bureau of Prisons, 2002).

To become a federal correctional officer the minimum education requirement is a four year college degree, or 3 years of related work experience or a combination of undergraduate education and work experience to equal three years of experience. At the end of 1999, only about 15 percent had an undergraduate degree, some graduate school or a graduate degree, while almost half (49.3%) had a high school diploma. Additionally, almost one third (32.7%) had some college. This clearly shows than most officers had prior correctional officer experience or a combination of some college and prior work experience before being hired by the Bureau of Prisons.

The Federal Bureau of Prisons divides the United States into six geographical regions; Northeast, North Central, Mid-Atlantic, Southeast, South Central and West. Almost one -fifth (19.2%) of all federal correctional officers work in the Northeast region, 17. 5 percent work in the North Central region, 15.3 work in the Mid Atlantic region, 17. 5 work in the Southeast region, 17.9 percent work in the South Central region and 12.3 percent work in the West. Most female correctional officers (23.5%) work in the South Central region while most male officers (19.7%) work in the Northeast area. Three of every ten black female federal correctional officers work in the Southeast region, whereas 31 percent of black male federal correctional officers work in the Southeast region. Almost one in five white female federal correctional officers works in the South Central region while almost one in four white male federal correctional officers works in the North Central region. About half (47%) of all Hispanic male federal correctional officers work in either the South Central or West regions of the country, and over half (51.6%) of all Hispanic female federal correctional officers work in these same two regions of the country. Table 3.1 details the officers' educational levels.

State Correctional Officers

The examination of entire systems, individual units or several facilities in a system is dependent upon what topic a researcher is exploring. Variables such as age, race, gender, educational level, marital status, length of service, rank, and location can have an impact on such factors as stress (Cheek & Miller,

TABLE 3.1
EDUCATION OF FEDERAL CORRECTIONAL OFFICERS
2002

EDUCATIONAL LEVEL	PERCENTAGE	NUMBER
Less than high school	0.3	44
High school graduate	49.3	7282
Technical School	3.1	459
Some college	32.7	4822
College degree	13.2	1941
Some graduate school	0.7	108
Master's degree	0.8	90
Ph.D. degree	<0.05%	3

Source: Bureau of Justice Statistics. (2003). *Sourcebook of Criminal Justice Statistics, 2002.* Washington, D.C.: U.S. Department of Justice.

1983; Grossi & Berg, 1991; Gross, Larson, Urban & Zupan, 1994), job satisfaction (Jurik, 1984; Jurik, Halemba, Musheno & Boyle, 1987; Walters, 1993), attitudes toward inmates (Jurik, 1985), attitudes toward treatment programs for inmates (Jackson & Ammen (1994), the working orientation of the officer (Whitehead, Lindquist & Klofas, 1987; Cullen, Lutze, Link & Wolfe, 1989; Robinson, Porporino & Simourd, 1993; Walters, 1995), and officer discretion (Klofas, 1986).

One of the richest sources of information about state correctional officers in one system is Patenaude and Golden's (2000) study of the Arkansas Department of Corrections. The focus of the study was the retention of officers but ample demographic data were also gathered. Questionnaires were sent to all CO I's and CO II's in the system with a return rate of all most 50 percent. Almost two-thirds (63.3%) of the respondents were African-American, and 56 percent were male. The average age of CO I's and CO II's was 33.5 years of age with a range of 18 to 64 years. An examination of the variables age and race reveals that older officers are more likely to be white males. In examining all ranks of officers, Patenaude and Golden (2000) reported that 29 percent were white males, 7. 7 percent white females, 30.9 percent black males and 32.4 percent black females. There were more black female officers in the system than any other group. Most of the officers in Arkansas were married (49.7%), while almost 3 in 10 (28.5%) were single, and 15.4 percent were divorced. When examining marital status and race, results were similar for both groups. Seventeen percent of whites and 14 percent of blacks reported their marital status as divorced. More blacks (37 %), than whites (12%) however, indicated their marital status as single or never married. When the authors reviewed educational levels subtle differences between races were evident. Overall, about half of the officers had a high school diploma while almost 40 percent had some college and over 8 percent had a college degree. Blacks were more likely than whites to have attended college, 41 percent as opposed to 34 percent. Forty five black officers compared to 22 white officers possessed college degrees.

The average length of service in the Arkansas Department of Corrections was 3. 8 years. The longest length of service was 24 years with the median length being two years. Almost two-thirds of these correctional officers had been with the Department of Corrections for less than three years. Half of those officers had worked for the Department a year or less. The final demographic variable examined by Patenaude and Golden (2000) was travel distance to work. They reported that most of the units in the system were located in rural areas surrounded by large-acreage tracts. In fact, the average one-way distance driven by a correctional officer was slightly more than 22 miles. This means that close to 10,000 miles a year were to traveled to work. The longest drive for one officer was 88 miles one-way. An overly simplistic review of Patenaude and Golden's

(2000) study reveals that the average correctional officer in Arkansas is a married black male in his early thirties with at least some college, employed by the Department for about 4 years, driving 22 miles one way to work in a rural prison. Research from other states reveal somewhat different findings.

Cullen, Link, Cullen and Wolfe (1990), and Cullen, Lutze, Link and Wolfe (1989) conducted research on job satisfaction by analyzing data obtained from a 1983 questionnaire sent to correctional officers in a southern correctional system. Such background characteristics as age, race gender, length of service, education and institutional security level were obtained from the 155 usable questionnaires (a 62% return rate). The background characteristics of the respondents were compared to characteristics of all officers working for that state. For most characteristics, the sample was comparable to the general population. The officer characteristics for this state indicate that the majority of the officers in the survey and within the department were males (79% and 82% respectively), who were about 37 years of age (38.1 versus 37 years old), employed by the department for 3 years (3.5 years versus 3 years), with about 1 year of college. The survey revealed that 57% of the officers were white, while the majority of the officers within this department in general were black (54%). The survey revealed that only 19 percent of those officers responding to the questionnaire were college graduates, while for the department as a whole the number was almost doubled (36%). About 42 percent of the surveyed officers and 48 percent of all officers work in a maximum security institution. Sampling error can account for the differences between those responding to the survey and the general population. This survey provides a small glimpse of the background characteristics of the officers working for one system. It is important to remember that the focus of this study was not on officer characteristics but on attitudes.

Another group of researchers who focused on officer attitudes were Jurik (1985) concerning officer attitudes toward inmates; Jurik and Halemba (1984) examining female officer attitudes; and Jurik, Halemba, Musheno and Boyle (1987) exploring job satisfaction and professionalization among correctional officers. These three groups of researchers utilized the same data set collected from 179 correctional officers working at a single institution in a state department of corrections in the western United States which they identify only as WDOC. Since the Jurik and Halemba (1984) article focused on female correctional officers all the demographic variables for that study were divided by gender. The discussion of demographic characteristics by the other two research groups were not differentiated by gender. Each group reported on different characteristics than did the other groups. Examining all three studies together can reveal a richness of detail that is not evident by reviewing these reports singularly.

In describing correctional officers, Jurik and Halemba (1984: 555) stated "the individuals interviewed at this facility did not fit the stereotype so frequently utilized in the media to characterize correctional officers. That is, as a group, they were not rural and uneducated 'good ole boys'." The facility in which these officers worked was a medium-minimum security facility, about two years old, located on the outskirts of a major metropolitan area. Line officers from all three shifts were involved in this research project. Sixty percent of the officers surveyed were hired to work directly in this facility while the other 40 percent transferred in from other facilities within the state. Results reveal that about 40 percent of the officers were between the ages of 26 and 35. Twenty two percent were between 18 and 25 years old, while 37 percent were older than 36. In examining the age distribution by gender the data reveal that about one in five males and one in four females were between the ages of 18 and 25. About the same percentage of males and females were between the ages of 26 and 35, while about one in three females but less than one in five males were between the ages of thirty-six and forty-five. Only in the over-46 age category were there substantially more males than females; 20 percent of the males were in this age

53

category while only 5 percent of the female officers were within this age group.

The vast majority of the officers (88%) working at this facility lived in populated urban areas east of their workplace (Jurik, 1985). Ninety five percent of the female officers listed their residence as urban, while for the male officers 87 percent resided in an urban area. Fifty three percent of the respondents indicated they were married, almost 25 percent were single, and the other 22 percent were divorced or separated. Only 25 percent of the females indicated they were married, whereas almost a third indicated they were single and 42.5 percent stated they were divorced or separated. Sixty percent of the males were married, 22 percent single, and only sixteen percent of the males indicated they were divorced or separated.

Several significant differences were noted between male and female officers. Seventy percent of the female officers with college degrees had degrees in areas other than criminal justice such as social welfare, sociology, psychology, counseling or education. About half of the college-educated male officers had degrees in criminal justice. About two-thirds of female offices, but less than half of the male officers reported that a parent was a professional, in a managerial position, or self employed. One of the most striking differences between the two groups centered on reasons for taking the job. In response to this question well over half (55%) of the females indicated they took the job because they were interested in human service work or in inmate rehabilitation. Less than one fourth (23%) of the males responded likewise, indicating female officers were more likely to have intrinsic reasons for seeking employment. Job security and a steady income did not rank high for either males or females. Salary as the reason for taking the job ranked third for females and sixth for males. While job security ranked third for males, it didn't even make the list for females. This counters conventional wisdom that job security and a steady pay check are the major drawing cards to the field of corrections.

Two other interesting differences were that almost 60 percent of the males but none of the females had served in the military and over two thirds of the males (68%) yet only 38 percent of the females had previous law enforcement experience. This study was conducted in the early 1980s, less than a decade after the creation of the all-volunteer armed forces and the widespread inclusion of females in law enforcement agencies. This could limit opportunities for females. Another explanation could center on the age of the officers involved in this survey. Almost one in four females were between the ages of 18 and 25 and about 75 percent had some college education. It is possible that more females went the education route than the service or law enforcement route.

Klofas (1986) examined background characteristics of correctional officers and officer discretion. Questionnaires were distributed to all officers working in four maximum security prisons in New York. The four facilities include: Ossining located near New York City, Auburn located southwest of Syracuse, Great Meadow prison in a semi-rural area, and Clinton, located in a rural area near the Canadian border "where few alternative sources of employment are available" (Klofas, 1986: 113). The racial composition of officers was reflective of the location of the prisons. At Ossining over two- thirds (68.8%) of the officers were black and 15.6 percent were Hispanic. Almost all of the officers in the other three prisons were white. This research challenged two popular stereotypes: that of old, white, rural prison guards - assumed to be unbending, and custodially minded - while his counterpart, the young, black, urban officer was assumed to be the opposite. The findings of this research revealed that there were no significant differences in interest in human services when race was considered and that human service interest increased with age. In other words, younger officers tended to be rigidly custodial (regardless of race or location), while age and experience leads to a more flexible outlook and an increase in providing discretionary human services.

In a study of officer attitudes toward inmate treatment programs, Jackson and Ammen (1996) compared a ten percent random sample of officers with the total population of correctional officers within the Texas Department of Criminal Justice - Institutional Division (formerly the Texas Department of Corrections or TDC). Statewide, about seventy six percent of the officers were male, about two thirds (64%) were white, one fourth were black and ten percent were Hispanic. The background characteristics of the officers involved in the sample reveal that the racial composition of the sample was reflective of the general population since two thirds were white and 78.8 percent were male. Over one quarter of the respondents indicated they had some college or a college degree. Most were married (63%), while about one in five were single, and one in eight were divorced. While the average age was 36 years, almost half (49%) were between 18 and 33 years of age. Almost the same percentage of officers were 49 and older (18%) as where those 18 to 25 (17%).

In a study of more than a 1,000 correctional officers in the Michigan Department of Corrections Gross, Larson, Urban and Zupan (1994) selected officers from all 25 institutional facilities and five camps to examine gender differences and occupational stress. The purpose was to determine if female officers experienced higher levels of stress than did male correctional officers. Numerous background variables were examined to determine if differences exited between genders. Examination of the demographic data reveal that seventy percent were males, thirty percent females, sixty-six percent white, twenty-eight percent black, and six percent other groups. Not only were background characteristics broken down by gender, but also by gender and race. While Whites accounted for seventy percent of all officers and over three-fourths (77%) of the white officers were male. Blacks accounted for 28 percent of all officers and almost half (47%) of all black officers were female. There were twice the percentage of black female officers than white female officers. For all officers, the average age was 35 with little difference between races or genders. As for length of service, the authors reported slight differences among the groups. About two-thirds (65.2%) of the black females and almost two-thirds (63.2%) of the white females had two or less years of seniority while slightly more than half (52.9%) of white males and about six of ten black males (58.2%) were employed for the same time period. The major differences between these groups become evident when seniority was 10 years or more. No black females and only 1.4 percent of black males had been with the system for that length of time. Over seven percent of all white males and 2.6 percent of white females had worked for the Michigan Department of Corrections ten or more years. It is evident in this study that the Department of Corrections had shifted its recruiting practice to recruit more women and minorities.

Regardless of race, males were more likely to be married than females. For white males, 70 percent were married with 56 percent married with children. Only about sixteen percent of the white males were single. Over half of the black males were married with 40 percent married with children. Twenty seven percent indicated they were single. As for the female officers, about a third (34.5%) of white female officers were married and slightly more than one-quarter (27.9%) of the black female officers were married. Forty percent of black females and twenty one percent of the white females were identified as being single. More white female officers were widowed (35.8%) than married (34.5%). Age may be affecting marital status in this survey. Almost three-fourths of all white females were over 30 years of age and twenty five percent were over the age of forty. Since about 90 percent of the white females had been employed less than five years it might be hypothesized that many females started with the department after the loss of a spouse.

Walters' (1993) study of almost 700 correctional officers working at four different prisons in a midwestern state focused on gender and job satisfaction. Background information on officers in this study revealed seventy-eight percent were male and twenty-two percent female. The average age was 41 years old and the average length of service with this organization was 51 months. Almost all (90%) of the officers were white. Seventy percent of all officers indicated their marital status as unmarried. Females were more likely to work at the minimum security prison, the women's prison, or the reception center, rather than at the maximum security facility.

Cheek and Miller's (1983) research on correctional officer stress utilized both state and county officers attending regular ongoing programs of the New Jersey Correction Officers Training Academy during the late 1970s. One hundred forty three usable questionnaires were completed by officers in 12 different classes. The results of this study were similar to those reported above. The vast majority of officers were male (87%). Seventy eight percent were white, twenty percent black and two percent other groups. The largest group of the officers in this survey (41%) were under the age of thirty, while one-third were over the age of forty. The large percentage of older officers might be indicative of the fact that two-thirds had more than 2 years experience and thirty percent of these officers held the rank of sergeant or higher. Half the officers in this survey were married, while 27% were single, 11% were divorced or separated, and 12% had remarried. Fifty-eight percent had some college and seven percent had college degrees.

Kauffman, in her study of correctional officers at Massachusetts' maximum security prison at Walpole, found that although most inmates came from the Boston area, the officers did not. Walpole is located in a rural community about twenty miles southwest of Boston. Most of the officers came from "small towns and communities of southeast Massachusetts down to the old whaling ports of New Bedford and Fall River" (1988: 31). She goes on to state "Many were immigrants or sons of immigrants, but few were members of racial minority groups" (Kauffman, 1988: 31).

Lombardo (1989), in his study of correctional officers at New York's maximum security prison in Auburn, a small rural area about 25 miles southwest of Syracuse, reported that 75% of the officers working there were born in the community surrounding the prison. The majority of employees previous work experience were blue collar factory or construction jobs.

Jacobs (1977) examined Stateville, Illinois' maximum security prison located about 50 miles southwest of Chicago, also reported that many officers were from rural areas of Illinois. According to Jacobs (1977: 40), Joseph Ragen (warden from 1936-1961) "recruited guards exclusively from rural southern Illinois". Officers were not attracted to Stateville "by any special desire to work in a prison, but left their homes to escape a dismal economic situation that had plagued southern Illinois for decades."

Correctional Officers in Jails

Commonly ignored, county jails hold a significant number of American inmates. Almost one-third of all inmates reside in jails, and these institutions range in size from very small to the largest correctional facilities in the country. While a limited number of jails are operated by states and the federal government, most are operated by counties under the auspices of the county sheriff. Sheriffs are unique in that they are both law enforcement officers and correctional administrators. This dual nature of sheriff's departments can result in some jail staffing issues. Many times jail security is seen by many sheriff's deputies as a task they must endure to become road officers and do "real" police work. Neither by vocation nor training are they really interested in correctional work. Some jurisdictions hire correctional officers, non-sworn personnel, to act in the role as jailer. These individuals have chosen to work in corrections, and may or may not desire to become police officers. Sheriffs prefer differing types of personnel for a variety of reasons. Some reasons for their preferences are displayed in Table 3.3.

TABLE 3.2
CHARACTERISTICS OF CORRECTIONAL OFFICERS
EMPLOYED IN JAILS 1999

	total	white	black	hispanic	other	na	male	female
U.S.	141,663	83,920	33,583	10,994	1,611	11,555	101,859	39,804
Federal	1685	602	454	563	61	5	1,408	277
State & Local	139,978	83,318	33,129	10,431	1,550	11,550	100,451	39,527

Source: Bureau of Justice Statistics. (2003). *Sourcebook of Criminal Justice Statistics 2002.* Washington, D.C.: U.S. Department of Justice.

TABLE 3.3
SHERIFFS' JAIL STAFFING PREFERENCES

REASON	PREFER DEPUTIES n=24	PREFER COs n=34	PREFER USING BOTH n=3
Better trained	41.7%	32.4%	
More versatile	58.3%	5.9%	66.7%
Less expensive		32.4%	
Fewer Union Problems		5.9%	
Want to work in jail		20.6%	
Other		2.9%	33.3%

Source: Walters, Stephen. (1994). "Jail Security Officer Training: The Perceptions of County Sheriffs". *Journal of Correctional Officer Training* (Summer:) 4-8, 19-24.

60

Summary

As indicated by the afore-mentioned studies, it is difficult to generalize about contemporary correctional officers. Differences exist throughout the country as well as within an individual system. The average officer today could be male or female, black, white, Hispanic, or other. They may be married or single, divorced or separated, high school graduate or holder of a bachelor's or even a graduate degree. The officer may come from a rural or urban area, may live close by or drive many miles to work. They may have chosen to be correctional officers for the pay, or for job security, or because of a desire to help others. No one group holds a monopoly on the title of correctional officer. Correctional officers are just as varied as employees in any other occupation in this country. The days of the 'good ole boys' are long gone.

4

CORRECTIONAL OFFICERS, INMATES, & SOCIAL CONTROL

Perhaps the most legendary of interpersonal relationships in the criminal justice system concerns correctional officers and prison inmates. The interaction between COs and inmates has habitually been characterized by the media as one fraught with constant violence, abuse, and exploitation by sadistic guards victimizing defenseless, noble inmates. Yet in reality this rather slanderous stereotypical characterization has little justification. As previously noted, correctional officers are generally vastly outnumbered by inmates, and the reality of prison operation, along with legal and professional constraints, make the media's representation of prison life inaccurate at best.

Unfortunately, some of these misconceptions may have been inadvertently encouraged by social scientists. One well-known study of a "simulated prison" is a case in point (Haney, Banks, and Zimbardo, 1973). This interesting research utilized college students to play the roles of both prison guards and prison inmates in a setting designed to simulate those found in a correctional environment. It was found that during the course of this experiment many of the students assigned to the role of guard became abusive, and developed feelings of enhanced social power and social status. Some appeared to enjoy the power and control that they wielded over the inmate group. The interaction between the two groups was characterized as "negative, hostile, affrontive, and dehumanizing" (Haney, Banks, and Zimbardo, 1973: 80). Students assigned to the role of inmate became generally passive, and several were "released" from the experiment early as they were beginning to develop signs of serious psychological distress. As a result, the experiment was terminated earlier than planned. Regardless of how similar this scenario may appear to prison life, there were important differences. The students assigned to the role of guard received no training. There were no rules that defined which behaviors were appropriate or inappropriate. And real-life prison inmates are certainly not passive, naive college students. In short, little in this study truly approximates prison life.

In reality, the social interaction between correctional officers and prison inmates is far more complex. The first well-known scholarly work to examine the dynamics of the daily interplay between COs and inmates was *The Society of Captives* by Gresham Sykes (1958). Rather than a system of total power of keepers over the kept, Syke's observed that CO - inmate relationships were characterized by both conflict and reciprocity. Guards cannot ensure inmate compliance by force. Force is limited in its ability to make inmates complete complex tasks, like working in a prison industry. Furthermore, COs are always greatly outnumbered by inmates and, unknown to most civilians, unarmed while working within the correctional facility. Punishments that are available, such as restrictions on visitation, removal of commissary privileges, etc., are feeble at best and make no marked difference in most inmates' behavior. Inmates do not see these privileges as something to be earned but rather as rights to which they are entitled. Inmates therefore have nothing to gain by compliance, only the possibly of "punishment" if they do not. COs lack any real punishments, and no rewards with which to induce inmate conformity.

Sykes also noted that the social system of the prison serves to complicate the relationships of correctional officers and their inmate charges. COs and inmates live in the same world and are constantly interacting. Most people want to get along with one another and the constant abuse, ridicule, and destain that inmates may display toward COs is something that most would prefer to avoid. Living together intimately in a closed prison society may also cause officers to see inmates as people rather than merely as inmates, and this can complicate the "ideal" relationship of separateness between the two groups. Added to these pressures is an administration that desires a smoothly-operating institution, and that does not want problems with the inmate population. Thus, COs are many times forced to bend rules or make deals with inmates in order to gain their compliance and avoid conflict. Rule breaking may be tolerated in some areas to enable to officer to be able to enforce rules in other areas. This opens the CO to blackmail by inmates who threaten to expose their past indiscretions to the officer's superiors. Furthermore, the workload of correctional officers is such that in many instances they are forced to rely on the assistance of inmates to see that the prison runs smoothly. Inmates are therefore able to leverage COs with the threat to withhold compliance, making the job of the officer all the more difficult. All of these factors have come to be referred to as the "corruption of authority." Sykes (1958: 61) summarized the problem:

> *The lack of a sense of duty among those who are held captive, the obvious fallacies of coercion, the pathetic collection of rewards and punishments to induce compliance, the strong pressures toward the corruption of the guard in the form of friendship, reciprocity, and the transfer of duties into the hands of trusted inmates - all are structural defects in the prison's system of power rather than individual inadequacies* (italics original).

The Inmate World

Inmates are forced involuntarily into a world not of their making. The prison subculture is a subculture of criminals. Fundamentally an antisocial world at best, living amongst the criminal element can be a nasty and brutish business. While many of the difficulties that are encountered by inmates in their correctional careers are personal in nature, others are the result of structural phenomena endemic to operating a correctional facility. Inmates must cope with these impediments, and in doing so may run afoul of their CO supervisors. These difficulties have been referred to as the "pains of imprisonment" (Sykes, 1958). The most obvious of these is the *deprivation of liberty*. Inmates are unable to leave. The world goes on without them and they are helpless to change their situation, short of escape. The "real world" of free civilians may be geographically close, but it is sociologically remote. The universe of an inmate is bounded by either walls or fences, and these barriers are not only physical, they are psychological. The inmate cannot leave without risk of life, and it is the correctional officer who is an essential component of this isolation.

Inmates also endure the *deprivation of autonomy*. Prisons would be unable to operate if inmates were to choose for themselves what they wanted to do and when they wanted to do it. Therefore, as in all group living situations, most decision-making is removed from inmates and put in the hands of the prison administration. It is left to COs to enforce these rules, which sometimes can be quite restrictive. Inmates are told what to wear, when to eat, what to eat, when to recreate, when to have visitors, and what they may or may not have in their cells. This type of regimentation can be quite onerous for people who have been raised in a society that values individuality, but is requisite for the smooth operation of a correctional facility.

The *deprivation of goods and services* is another of the pains of imprisonment enumerated by Sykes. For security reasons most prisons put severe limitations on the amount and type of possessions that inmates are allowed to have. Officers conduct periodic searches, or shakedowns, to ferret out contraband. Yet the law of supply and demand remains a constant in the prison just as it does in the civilian world, and thus an underground economy develops. Alcohol, drugs, sex, pornography, clothing, weapons, etc., all are in demand by inmates. Other inmates attempt to satisfy this demand, and are thus placed in conflict with correctional officers whose duty it is to stamp out this underground trade

In an apparent paradox, Sykes notes that in a maximum security prison a *deprivation of security* exists. However, further consideration shows how true this is. American society incarcerates the most violent of its citizens, crowding them into what many times are substandard living conditions. Predatory criminals do not cease their predation simply because they have been imprisoned, rather they simply shift their target from the general population to the prison population. Violence, therefore, becomes an everyday concern for most inmates. This may entail proactive strikes against suspected protagonists and attempts to acquire weapons for defense. Violence among inmates is a continual problem for COs, who are required by statute to protect inmates in their custody. The magnitude of this problem is illustrated in Table 4.1.

TABLE 4.1
INMATE - INMATE VIOLENCE 1995/2000

	1995	2000
Inmate Assaults	25,948	34,355
Resulting Deaths	82	51

Source: Bureau of Justice Statistics. (2001). *Census of State and Federal Correctional Facilities, 2000.* Washington, D.C.: U.S. Department of Justice.

A final, unfortunate reality of inmate life is the *deprivation of heterosexual relationships*. While considered by most Americans to be an acceptable cost for criminal behavioral, it becomes a real problem for both inmates and the officers who supervise them. Consensual homosexual relationships violate prison rules that COs must enforce, while coerced sexual encounters are a constant threat to inmates. This threat leads to untold violent encounters in the prison environment.

Inmates are thus left to find ways to adapt to these prison realities, and many of these forms of adaptation may lead them into confrontation with the correctional officer staff. Several options are available to inmates (Bartollas, 1981). The *aggressive reaction* to confinement involves fighting the system by flouting it's rules and regulations for acceptable behavior, and sometimes physically assaulting COs (see Table 4.2). This type of adaptation unfortunately will bring the inmate into repeated conflict with COs, making the officers lives more miserable, and perhaps resulting in a loss of goodtime credit or a stint in administrative segregation.

TABLE 4.2
INMATE - STAFF VIOLENCE 1995/2000

	1995	2000
Inmate Assaults	14,165	17,952
Resulting Deaths	14	5

Source: Bureau of Justice Statistics. (2001). *Census of State and Federal Correctional Facilities, 2000*. Washington, D.C.: U.S. Department of Justice.

Other inmates may choose to fight the correctional system through protest in concert with other inmates, the *collective reaction*. This may indeed bring about some change that inmates find desirable, but may also result in prolonged imprisonment and increased hostility from officers. An increasingly popular inmate reaction to confinement has been the *legalistic reaction*. This methodology employs the legal system to improve the inmate's lot. For a period of time this mode of adaption showed promise for inmates, and resulted in several important changes in prison operation that will be discussed later in this chapter. Some inmates have elected to cope with prison life utilizing the *withdrawal reaction*. This mode of adaptation can operate in several ways. Alcohol and drugs can effectively serve to blunt the everyday oppression of prison life. While contraband, these substances are available to inmates who are willing to pay the price for their acquisition. Inmates may also request an assignment to Protective Custody if they desire to withdraw from the prison subculture. Yet "PC" allows little freedom, and inmates who reside there are generally despised by other inmates for their perceived weakness. Many inmates who "PC up" are the first targets of inmate reprisals during riots. Even less healthy forms of withdrawal for the incarcerated are mental illness and suicide. Psychologically removing oneself from the reality of prison life can be an effective, if pathological, way of dealing with its constant fear and degradation. Taking this response to its ultimate, ending what may be perceived as an intolerable existence is always an option, and correctional officers receive a great deal of training in dealing with this eventuality.

Other, less negative coping options are available to inmates. The *self-satisfying reaction* involves an inmate making the best of a bad situation by making prison life as comfortable as possible. Getting a good prison job, acquiring desired contraband, and acquiring status within the inmate community are all ways in which inmates can ameliorate their situation. Unfortunately, these same activities may bring an inmate into conflict with supervising COs. A final methodology, the *positive reaction*, is also a possibility. Most prisons offer a variety of programs that inmates can utilize to change their lives for the better. Academic and vocational training, drug and alcohol abuse programs - all are available to those inmates who wish to avail themselves of these opportunities. Unfortunately, considering the high rates of recidivism in American prisons, too few inmates make this choice.

Correctional Officer Responses

Given the previously discussed insufficiency of relying totally upon coercion as an inmate control methodology, COs must find other ways to ensure compliance from inmates. One study observed that the manner in which correctional officers chose to gain cooperation from inmates was, to a certain extent, dictated by their position in the officer hierarchy (Jacobs and Retsky, 1980). Lower ranking, newer correctional officers had a tendency to cope with inmates by attempting to become personable with them. Direct use of coercive power was not common, probably because both inmates and COs were aware that lower ranking officers in reality wielded little actual power or authority. Other officers, either because they had gained seniority or had been promoted to the rank of sergeant, found other ways to cope. Common among these officers was a tendency to find duty stations that removed them from direct contact with inmates. Administrative jobs, or perimeter security posts were preferred. Only those COs who had attained the rank of lieutenant or above relied on their power to coerce compliance from inmates, and these were generally the only officers who had enough power to actually do so.

Power, however, can take many forms (French and Raven, 1959). Successful correctional officers learn which form to use and when to use it. Most of the preceding discussion has focused on two types of power, *coercive power* and *reward power*. In a correctional setting, coercive power rests on the ability of the correctional officer being able to punish an inmate if that inmate fails to comply with the officer's directives. As we have seen, COs many times fail to have the required ability to actually punish an inmate with any sufficiency to force compliance. Most punishments available to officers, such as restrictions on commissary purchases, recreational programs, visitation, etc., are in fact feeble at best. Reward power, on the other hand, relies upon an officer being able to supply outcomes desirable to an inmate in return for the inmate's cooperation. Yet as Sykes has already noted, most rewards are given to an inmate *en mass* upon entry into the prison, thus removing them as possible positive outcomes for complying with the wishes of the correctional staff. As a result, many correctional officers fail to see either of these forms of power as particularly effective (Sykes, 1958; Hepburn, 1985).

Another form of power available to correctional officers is *legitimate power*. Legitimate power rests on inmates accepting the idea that COs have the right, because of their position, to demand inmate cooperation. Inmates comply with CO demands because they understand that they have an obligation to do so. Whether or not legitimate power is an effective inmate motivator is questionable, given the obvious fact that inmates wouldn't be inmates if they had any respect for legitimate authority. *Referent power* is another possibility for correctional officers, and may, in some rare instances, be useful. This type of power results when an inmate perceives a great deal of similarity between him/herself and the correctional officer. The perceived similarity creates a feeling of solidarity for the inmate, and increases the probability that cooperation will ensue. This hypothesis has been used to augment the case for the increased hiring of minority COs to more accurately mirror the racial and ethic profile of inmates in American prisons. However, the polarization in most prisons between inmates and COs makes this type of power of dubious utility.

This leaves *expert power* for officers to use. Expert power exists in a correctional setting when inmates realize that some COs have knowledge and information that the inmates need. Thus, officers who have expert power can gain compliance from an inmate because the inmate is dependent upon the officer. For example, many inmates have little or no correctional experience. Some information about prison life may be gained through interaction with other inmates. However, their fellow inmates may be of little assistance when it comes to understanding prison rules, regulations, and procedures. They may need assistance in gaining access to such things as caseworkers, visitation, commissary, and medical help. In jails, COs can be source of information about court procedures and possible court outcomes. Correctional officers can use their knowledge as a bargaining chip in a *quid pro quo* relationship with inmates, with both sides gaining from the interaction.

Forms and Functions of Physical Coercion

Physical coercion, however, can still be a viable tool for correctional officers, not only for the control of inmates, but also as a means of becoming a part of the subculture of correctional officers. James Marquart (1986) observed that COs in a Texas penitentiary used physical force in a highly structured and systematic manner. Three forms of physical coercion were available to officers. The first, referred to as "counseling", an "attitude adjustment", or a "tuneup", was used in cases of minor inmate infractions. These infractions might include disobeying an order, arguing with an officers, or having a bad attitude. The resulting officer reactions included shoving, kicks, and slaps. The physical damage incurred by the inmate was minimal, as this form of physical coercion was meant to mostly intimidate the inmate.

The second form of physical coercion was called an "ass whipping". This was a more serious activity, and was used when inmates challenged a COs authority, threatened an officer, or for fighting back during a "tune-up". Weapons were commonly employed by COs, such as batons, blackjacks, or flashlights. Even so, inmates were seldom harmed sufficiently to require extensive medical treatment. This may not have been the case with the final form of force, the "severe beating." The severe beating was meted out to inmates who attempted to escape, attacked COs, or incited other inmates to disobey officers. The goal here was serious physical injury, and thus could result in the hospitalization of the inmate. Most of the time, all three types of physical coercion occurred out of the sight of other inmates in order to avoid witnesses, but there were occasions when they were acted out publicly in order to make an example of an inmate.

Marquart observed that physical coercion served four functions for correctional officers. The first, and most obvious, is that physical coercion functions to aid COs in maintaining control and order within the institution. Officers were loath to allow inmates any opportunity to break rules and threaten either COs or other inmates. Officers were constantly outnumbered by inmates, and consequently felt the need to display dominance over inmates in order to retain internal control of the prison. Physical coercion also served to maintain the status of the officers and to ensure deference from inmates. In order to maintain order, COs felt it imperative that they retain the "respect" of inmates. Any attempt at disrespect, resistance, or antagonism by inmates was met with physical force. Inmates needed to be kept "in their place" if a smoothly operating prison was to result. In addition, coercion also served as a route to upward mobility for correctional officers. The ability and willingness to fight inmates was viewed as a positive attribute by supervisors, and functioned almost as a "rite of passage" for newer officers. COs who were willing to utilize coercive force were officers who could be trusted. Force was thought to be a legitimate social control mechanism, and the ability to properly utilize coercion was seen as a critical factor in the advancement of an officer's career. Finally, the use of coercive force by COs operated as a mechanism for building solidarity within the correctional officer corps. COs who used physical force were shown to have internalized the code that legitimized such behavior. These officers enjoyed high morale and low turnover rates. They could be trusted to maintain the secrecy of these illicit-force activities in the face of outside investigations. In short, these COs became members of the "hard core" of officers who were seen as successful.

Variation Among Correctional Officers

Research into the CO world has shown that variations do exist among correctional officers on a number of issues, including the issues of using force with inmates and in their general attitude toward inmates in general. Marquart (1986) observed, for example, that not all officers were equally likely to utilize physical force as a mechanism of social control. Younger COs, and those COs who newer at the job, were more likely to use coercive force. These officers were under constant pressure to prove themselves, and show that they could perform the job. Older, higher ranking officers had already established themselves, and thus were not under similar pressure. Furthermore, white officers were more likely to employ physical force than were either black or Hispanic officers.

Variation among correctional officers also exists in their general attitudes toward inmates. The literature commonly dichotomizes COs into two groups - those who are *custody oriented*, who feel that the main role of a CO is to function as the "police" within the prison; as opposed to those who are *treatment/rehabilitation oriented*, and perceive their role as a more human service activity.

Previous research with American correctional officers has uncovered several factors that are related to an officer having a custody orientation toward his/her profession. Higher levels of education have been found to lessen the probability that an officer will possess a custody orientation (Rogers, 1991; Poole and Regoli, 1980a; Teske and Williamson, 1979). Several studies reveal that custody oriented officers are characterized by a greater length of experience as correctional officers (Cullen et al., 1989; Jurik, 1985; Poole and Regoli, 1980a; Teske and Williamson, 1979), although research by Klofas and Toch (1982) reached the opposite conclusion. The age of a correctional officer has also proven to be important, with younger officers being more custody oriented and older officers less so (Jurik, 1985; Klofas and Toch, 1982; Teske and Williamson, 1979). In a related vein, Cullen et al. (1989) noted that the older an individual was when beginning work as a correctional officer, the more likely he/she would take a human service approach, rather than a custody approach, to their profession.

Race was also determined to have an affect on custody orientation. Several studies observed that minority officers were more in favor of rehabilitation and more positive toward inmates (Cullen et al., 1989; Jurik, 1985) and that whites appeared more punitive in their attitudes (Whitehead and Lindquist, 1989), although the latter research did note that white officers preferred less social distance from inmates than did black officers. Indeed, Jacobs and Kraft (1978) found that white officers were less punitive toward inmates than were minority officers. Role conflict/role stress was determined to characterize those officers who were custody oriented (Cullen et al., 1989; Poole and Regoli, 1980x). Male officers were found to be more custody oriented (Walters, 1992), while those officers who were retired military, held lower rank in the prison hierarchy, or who attended church were more inclined toward rehabilitation (Teske and Williamson, 1979). The research concerning the relationship between the security level in which an officer works and his/her custody orientation is contradictory. Jurik (1985) determined that officers who worked in minimum security environments were more positive toward inmates, while Smith and Hepburn (1979) found minimum security staff to be more punitive. Jurik (1985) observed those officers whose motivation for taking their job as a correctional officer was "intrinsic" in nature held attitudes more positive toward inmates. Finally, Cullen et al. (1989) revealed that those officers who worked the night shift, and those who received greater amounts of supervisory support, were more likely to be custody oriented.

Differential attitudes toward inmates among COs is not just a phenomenon common to American prisons. Several international and cross-cultural studies have been done that examine custody oriented correctional officers. Shamir and Drory (1981), examining Israeli prison officers, determined that officers who were less interested in rehabilitation were characterized by more role conflict, had greater amounts of correctional experience, and held high rank within the prison hierarchy. In another study of Israeli officers, Shamir and Drory (1982) observed that those officers who held hostile or punitive attitudes toward inmates exhibited more role conflict and less job satisfaction.

In a comparison of Korean and American correctional officers, Chang et al. (1990) revealed that both groups viewed inmates negatively. However, American officers viewed inmates as more undependable than did the Korean officers.

Burton et al. (1991), in a comparison of Bermudian and American officers, determined that increased education and increased income were positively related to Bermudian officers' pro-rehabilitation attitudes, while increased rank was negatively related to these same attitudes. Further, increased income levels were related to pro-custody attitudes among the Bermudian officers. In comparing American officers to those employed in Bermuda, the authors observed that the Bermudian officers showed more support for rehabilitation, were supportive of increased funding for rehabilitation programs, and were more sympathetic toward inmates.

In research examining Australian correctional officers, Williams (1983) found officers who were custody oriented were more likely to rely on disciplinary authority. These officers were also more likely to hold negative attitudes concerning inmates and to feel greater antagonism toward noncustodial prison staff. A second study of Australian correctional officers (Williams and Soutar, 1984) determined that officers in maximum security prisons were more likely to prefer a custodial role and to negatively stereotype inmates than were officers in other types of prisons.

Two studies of Taiwanese correctional officers revealed many similarities between Taiwanese and American officers (Chien-Yang, 1991; Huang, 1993). Huang (1993) observed that those officers holding higher rank were more concerned with security. In addition, officers who worked all cell blocks were more likely to score high on a "get tough" scale, those who had more training were more likely to be skeptical of rehabilitation, those who had suffered more assaults favored more security, and those who had taken their job as a means to take care of their family were also more security oriented. Conversely, this research determined that older officers, female officers, those who had support from their families for their job, and those who took chose their job for reasons of public service, all had less interest in custody and security. In addition, those officers with higher educational levels reflected less desire to "get tough".

Three studies analyzed Canadian correctional officers. Lagace (1994) noted that custody oriented male officers were less accepting of women as coworkers in prison. In a comparative study of Canadian and Indian correctional officers, Sandu (1972) found that among both groups increased age was related to a more favorable view of inmates. Among Canadian officers increased formal education was found to be related to a belief that inmates are amenable to rehabilitation. However, among Indian officers in-service training was related to the same belief. Robinson et al. (1993) observed that correctional officers were less supportive of rehabilitation than were case management staff. In addition, factors such as having a favorable attitude toward the field of corrections, being interested in career development, preferring to work with people, and desiring employment that allows for personal growth were all related to a support for rehabilitation. The authors also note that having an interest in security does not necessarily preclude an interest in rehabilitation.

Preferring a custody orientation to the correctional officer role can have important consequences for both the officer and for the prison environment in which he/she functions. These officers have been found to exhibit alienation from the workplace (Walters, 1991; Poole and Regoli, 1981). Officers who are custody oriented appeared to be more dissatisfied with their work than were those who had a more favorable attitude toward inmates (Cullen et al., 1985; Jurik and Halemba, 1984). Custody oriented officers wrote more disciplinary reports (Poole and Regoli, 1980a), yet still manifested higher levels of powerlessness (Walters, 1988). Poole and Regoli (1980b) observed that officers with poorer relations with inmates were more cynical. And in addition, custody oriented male officers were found to be less accepting of women as coworkers in the prison (Walters, 1993a).

Legal Constraints on Correctional Officers

As noted earlier in this chapter, correctional officers are subject to a variety of institutional rules and legal constraints when dealing with inmates in their custody. Although these rules are sometimes ignored, as we have seen in some cases of physical coercion, CO interaction with inmates is generally well-regulated.

This was not always the case (Archambeault and Archambeault, 1982). For a long period of time the courts were loathe to interfere in the operation of correctional facilities. Operating under what became to be known as the *Hands-Off Doctrine*, judges were hesitant to intervene in prison operation for three reasons. First, the judiciary had a great deal of respect for the principle of separation of powers which characterizes the American system of law. Prisons were rightly perceived as the purview of the executive branch, and thus interference by the judicial branch was seen as untoward. Second, judges during this period realized that they had no expertise in prison administration, and therefore were simply unqualified to intercede in prison operations. Finally, judges rightly determined that intervention into correctional procedures by the judiciary might serve to subvert the power of prison administrators and thus endanger the security of the prison. The epitome of this philosophy can be seen in the case *Ruffin v. the Commonwealth of Virginia* (1871), where the Courts ruled that inmates were effectively nothing more than slaves of the state.

By the 1960s the attitude of the judiciary toward prison administration changed drastically, and a new doctrine, the *Involved-Hands Doctrine*, became popular. This period of legal thought was diametrically opposed to previous legal doctrine. Courts took the position that inmates *were not* slaves of the state, but rather had rights to physical security, minimal living standards, constitutionally guaranteed due process safeguards, and to challenge the conditions of their confinement in court. The courts developed a "balance of interest" concept in which correctional administrators were forced to base their administrative decisions based on both the needs of institutional security and individual offender rights. It was during this time period that inmate litigation reached its zenith.

Within ten years the judiciary realized the error of their ways and moved to the *Restrained-Hands Doctrine* when dealing with correctional matters. The courts now stated that inmates were not slaves, but neither were they fully-enfranchised citizens. One does not lose all rights after conviction and incarceration, but one does not necessarily retain the full panoply of citizen rights they enjoyed before incarceration. This final doctrine took a more even-handed approach toward balancing the needs of the prison to control inmates and the inmates' constitutional rights.

TABLE 4.3
CORRECTIONAL FACILITIES UNDER CONSENT DECREES 2000

REASON	ALL FACILITIES	STATE FACILITIES	PRIVATE FACILITIES
Totality of conditions	59	52	7
Ordered to limit population	145	119	26
Crowding	105	98	7
Visiting/mail/telephone	104	97	7
Accommodation of the disabled	95	91	4
Religion policies	93	88	5
Mental health treatment	91	86	5
Search policies	85	78	7
Fire hazards	83	75	8
Medical facilities	75	66	9
Disciplinary policies	45	38	7
Grievance policies	43	33	10
Staffing	43	34	9
Administrative segregation	41	34	7
Library services	38	33	5
Recreation	38	29	9
Inmate classification	34	25	9
Food service/nutrition	28	21	7
Counseling programs	23	14	9
Education	23	18	5
Other	22	21	1
total	357	324	33

Source: Bureau of Justice Statistics. (2001). *Census of State and Federal Correctional Facilities, 2000*. Washington, D.C.: U.S. Department of Justice.

Still, despite of this new judicial reticence, a large number of correctional facilities in the United States are operating under consent decrees, issued by federal judges, that are designed to protect the rights of the incarcerated population. These legal constraints are shown in Table 4.3. Most egregious forms of inmate social control that had characterized American prisons are long past. While various forms of flogging have had a long history of utilization in correctional institutions, their usage was legally banned in the United States by *Jackson v. Bishop* (1968). In reality, however, most states had stopped using such measures long before. The fact is that the ability of correctional officers to use force is highly regulated. Fisher et al. (1987) observes that COs are allowed to utilize force in four situations: 1) to defend themselves; 2) to defend or aid another; 3) to enforce institutional regulations; and 4) to prevent the commission of a crime, including an escape.

The most common form of force utilized by prison officers is *non-deadly force*. This type of force is used in a variety of situations (Fisher et al.; 1987). For example, COs are allowed to use non-deadly force to protect themselves, other inmates, or other persons from inmate assaults. However, officers are also expected to use "reasonable" force. This means that an officer is expected to use only the amount of force necessary to eradicate the threat of harm, but no more. The CO is also required to stop using force when the inmate is subdued. Non-deadly force can also be used by correctional officers in order to ensure compliance with institutional rules and regulations, although it is generally preferred that a verbal warning precede physical contact. Mechanical and chemical means can also be employed by COs to ensure inmate compliance, but again their usage must be reasonable given the circumstances.

There are occasions, albeit rare, where correctional officers are called upon to use *deadly force* to maintain control of inmates. In most cases, COs can utilize deadly force in two circumstances: to prevent a felony (generally including escapes), or to prevent an act that could result in serious bodily harm, including death, to themselves or to others (Fisher et al.; 1987). While this principle appears straightforward, there can be problematic situations. The so-called "fleeing felon rule" historically held that those who had committed a felony and were fleeing from authorities could be killed by police or prison officers. However, many correctional facilities, particularly jails, hold a significant number of inmates who are either simply awaiting trial or who have been convicted of misdemeanors. This can cause problems for COs who may be unable to properly classify an escaping inmate. The customary attitude toward fleeing criminals was changed, however, by *Tennessee v. Garner* (1985). This ruling held that deadly force can only be used when: 1) it is necessary to prevent an escape, and 2) the escapee poses a credible threat to the life or physical well-being of the officer or others. Given some of the legal problems involved, many correctional systems have limited their usage of deadly force to this second category of events.

Interestingly, correctional officers may be required to exercise force in two other general situations; to protect the inmate from other inmates, and to protect the inmate from him/herself (Fisher et al.; 1987). This duty can sometimes be a rather onerous one for a CO. It can be difficult for an officer to place him/herself in jeopardy to protect an inmate who may have verbal or physically abused the officer in the past. Nonetheless, when inmates are in the custody of the state, the state becomes responsible for their well-being. Failure to do so can result in civil liability for both the institution and perhaps the individual officer. An officer may therefore be required to use either type of force to protect the life and welfare of an inmate. By extension, COs are also required to protect inmates from themselves. As previously discussed, inmates may choose to deal with prison life by suicide, drug usage, mental problems, or self-mutilation. These acts can be injurious to the inmate, and even though they are instigated by the inmates themselves, many courts have ruled that prisons may be liable for damages if it can be shown that the COs acted in a negligent manner or if the institution had no policies in place to deal with such exigencies.

Summary

Contrary to the stereotypical relationship assumed by many, the interaction between correctional officers and inmates is quite complex. While we have seen that sometimes CO-inmate violence does occur, officers are certainly not free to roam about prisons inflicting random indignities upon helpless inmates. After all, inmates vastly outnumber correctional officers and generally have a history of violent behavior, and they have their own problems dealing with the deprivations of incarceration. Thus inmates would not tolerate such behavior, and COs would not be so adventurous as to forget this fact. This reality, combined with legal and professional constraints, renders the old stereotype obsolete. Rather, prison officers and inmates many times find themselves in a relationship of mutual interdependence.

5

THE SOCIAL PSYCHOLOGY OF CORRECTIONAL OFFICERS

When one takes into account the pressures correctional officers experience in the course of their duties, it is not surprising that many endure substantial psychological consequences. Conflicts with both inmates and administrators, constant threats to physical safety, a lack of input into the decision-making process, poor working conditions, a lack of appreciation for their work and a poor public image - all may result in officers who suffer from one of several forms of psychological malaise. Research has identified numerous social psychological difficulties that are commonly encountered by correctional officers as a consequence of their career. These include feelings of stress, burnout, alienation, role conflict, cynicism, and job dissatisfaction. These processes, sometimes individually, sometimes in interaction with others, can seriously affect COs as they attempt to maintain control of America's prison inmates. In fact, the pressures on correctional officers are so great that, on occasion, the result can be suicide.

Stress

Perhaps the most common of all the psychological problems that may be experienced by a correctional officer is stress. Spending one's career locked in a prison vastly outnumbered by convicted criminals, many of whom having committed the most violent of offenses, might reasonably generate a certain amount of stress in the most hardened of correctional officers. In fact, empirical studies have determined that correctional officers do suffer from higher levels of stress than does the "normal" non-correctional officer population (Cheek and Miller, 1982; Lasky et al., 1986). Perhaps indicative of these high stress rates, Moracco (1985) notes that COs have a divorce rate that is twice the national average and suffer one of the highest rates of heart attacks of state employees.

Stress has been defined as "a non-specific response to a perceived threat to an individual's well-being or self-esteem" (Moracco, 1985: 22). Stress is "non-specific" in that each individual may respond differently to its occurrence. These responses may be physical, psychological, or both. Further, stress is a *perceived* condition, in that a situation may be stressful to one individual but that same situation may not interpreted as stressful by another. The consequences of chronic stress for correctional officers can be both varied and serious. Physiologically stress can manifest itself in assorted ways, including elevated blood pressure, changes in weight, lack of sleep, nervousness, fatigue, and a variety of aches and pains. The psychological consequences of stress may entail increased irritability and inability to maintain concentration. Further, stress appears to interact with other social psychological processes important to understanding correctional officers, such as alienation, burnout, role conflict, and job dissatisfaction.

Given the importance of stress to the individual well-being of COs and their ability to function affectively in the prison environment, it is not surprising that it has received considerable attention from criminologists interested in correctional staffing. Cheek and Miller (1983) observed that while correctional officers suffer from high levels of stress, they are loath to admit it to others. This "John Wayne Syndrome" does not allow for COs to express their stress due to the "macho" image of their profession. Yet these same officers report that their fellow officers suffer from all forms of stress-related problems. In order of frequency, correctional officers observe that stress affects their co-workers' 1) emotional health, 2) physical health, 3) family relationships, and 4) job performance. These officers are likely to handle their stress by externalizing it through either aggressive or assertive responses toward those with whom they interact. Sadly, these COs also report that it is common for officers to "take their stress home", contributing to the high levels of family dysfunction among correctional officers previously alluded to.

Several criminologists have examined the relationship between *officer demographics* and the experience of stress in the correctional workplace. The age of a correctional officer has been hypothesized to be related to experiencing higher levels of stress. However, the findings are inconsistent at best. Both Blau et al. (1986) and Merlak and Hepburn (1992) found increasing age to be a shield against stress in the prison workplace. Perhaps the adage "older but wiser" is the key. Older COs may have developed more coping skills than their younger counterparts and thus are better able to cope with the stressful prison environment. Yet Lasky et al. (1986) found the opposite relationship to exist, with older officers suffering from higher stress levels than their younger co-workers. Perhaps these contradictory findings are a result of the differing prison environments under study; the first two having been done in state prisons while the latter was done in a federal prison. However, numerous studies in other occupational fields tend to support the idea that increased age lessens the experience of stress (Merlak and Hepburn, 1992).

An officer's gender also appears to be related to the probability of experiencing stress while working in prison. Women correctional officers have been found to suffer from higher levels of stress than do their male counterparts (Blau et al., 1986; Cheek and Miller, 1983; Cullen et al., 1985; Gross et al.; 1994). Jurik (1988) states that this increased stress may not only be the result of the normal stressors that affect all COs regardless of gender, but may also be the consequence of conflicts with male correctional officers on the job (see Chapter 7).

Race and ethnicity appear to have some affect on the level of stress endured by COs. Research shows that white correctional officers suffer higher levels of work stress than do non-white officers. In a study of several New York state prisons Blau et al. (1986) observed that both Black and Hispanic COs exhibited lower amounts of stress than did white co-workers. The authors hypothesized that the difference was attributable to the fact that the prisons under examination had an inmate majority that was non-white, thus non-white officers felt more secure and less stressed. However, the relationship between stress and race/ethnicity probably needs more study.

Marital status is another demographic variable that appears to be associated with stress among correctional officers. Interestingly, married officers appear more stressed than unmarried COs (Blau et al., 1986). Furthermore, in a related vein, a lack of family support has also been found to be a stressor (Cullen et al., 1985). Apparently when COs take their stress home with them it simply multiplies the damage.

A more fruitful line of inquiry into correctional officer stress looks to factors in *the prison work environment* for uncovering occupational stressors. One of the more common stressors of COs found by researchers is problems with the prison administration (Lasky et al., 1986; Cheek and Miller, 1982; Cullen et al. 1985). Correctional officers often feel there is a lack of communication between themselves and the correctional administration. COs spend eight hours a day in direct contact with inmates, yet few prison administrations allow COs any input into the decision-making process. Many officers anticipate conflict with inmates, but they also expect that when these conflicts occur the prison administration will back the officers completely. Unfortunately, there is an impression among some COs that this support is sadly lacking, adding to their levels of stress. As some correctional officers commented:

> "In this institution the administration does not stand behind the correctional officer, therefore adding to the stress and high turnover rate" (Walters, 1991: 56).

> ".... the main point is the administration is always trying to fuck us over in many ways like breaking the contract and not giving a shit about us" (Walters, 1985).

Conflict with the inmate population is also a powerful stressor for many correctional officers (Cheek and Miller, 1983; Cullen et al., 1985). COs are commonly bombarded with verbal abuse, disrespect, a lack of cooperation, and sometimes direct physical attack from the inmates they supervise. Inmates, who were unable to follow society's rules on the street, can make life difficult for officers who are responsible for enforcing prison rules. The effects of these conflicts over time, and the ever-present possibly of injury or even death, add to the stress of correctional work. Cheek and Miller (1983) report the two most stressful aspects of officer-inmate interaction involve inmate surveillance and inmate violence. Officers are required to observe inmate behavior in housing units, dining rooms, and corridors. In all of these situations COs are surrounded by large numbers of inmates who could, if they thought it was in their best interest, take control from the supervising officers. Inmate behavior can take the form of a variety of disturbances, including the stabbing of COs. In fact, Cheek and Miller (1983) observed that the most disliked and feared aspect of a correctional officer's job was the violence that they may encounter. Two correctional officers related the following feelings:

"When I first started here I was a little wary of inmates but now they know what to expect from me and I know what to expect from them. I really think there should be much more punishment than there is. I saw two officers get stabbed and the inmates who stabbed them walked out of the building unharmed. That really was too bad" (Walters, 1985).

"I was stabbed five times because I did my job and made the inmates follow the rules and never got buddy-buddy with the con bosses. I made them follow the rules like everyone else so they tried to kill me to try to get rid of me which worked, just showing the inmates run the prison" (Walters, 1985).

Several other stressors in the prison environment have been identified. Cullen et al. (1985) note that COs who are assigned to maximum security areas have higher levels of stress than do officers assigned to less secure areas. This sounds reasonable as the most aggressive and disruptive inmates are generally housed in maximum security units. However, neither Lasky et al. (1986) nor Blau et al. (1986) were able to find any variation in the degree of stress among officers assigned to differing security levels. Lasky et al. suggest this finding is the result of correctional officers "topping out" on stress scales, thus no significant variation is stress scores is possible. Stress can also be caused by an inability of correctional officers to see any positive results from their work. Inmates in general fail to change in any meaningful way on a time scale that is perceivable to COs. This may contribute to low staff morale, which has also been determined to be a correctional officer stressor. Finally, many COs feel that their negative job image among the general civilian population causes them significant stress (Cheek and Miller, 1982).

Unfortunately, evidence exists that stress among correctional officers is not ameliorated by increased experience on the job. On the contrary, it appears that the affects of stress may be additive, as some research has determined that increased tenure as a CO is related to increased levels of stress (Lasky et al., 1986; Cullen et al., 1985).

Burnout

Closely related to stress is the problem of "burnout" among correctional officers. While several definitions of burnout exist, most see burnout as a *process* that results from excessive stress in the workplace, particularly among human service workers such as correctional officers. Cherniss (1980: 17-18) describes burnout as a progressive problem involving stress, strain, and defensive coping:

> The first stage involves as imbalance between resources and demand (stress). The second stage is the immediate, short-term emotional tension, fatigue, and exhaustion (strain). The third stage consists a number of changes in attitude and behavior, such as a tendency to treat clients in a detached and mechanical fashion or a cynical preoccupation with the gratification of one's own needs (defensive coping). Burnout thus refers to a transactional process, a process consisting of job stress, work strain, and psychological accommodation. Specifically, burnout can now be defined as a process in which a previously committed professional disengages from his or her work in response to stress and strain experienced in the job.

Thus, burnout is not the same phenomenon as stress, rather it is the behavioral and psychological consequence of stress suffered in the workplace. Given the previously discussed problem of stress among correctional officers, it is not surprising that many COs also suffer from burnout. Hurst and Hurst (1997) examined 244 correctional officers employed in the Kentucky prison system utilizing the Maslach Burnout Inventory. This inventory measures three elements of burnout; emotional exhaustion, depersonalization, and feelings of a lack of personal accomplishment. Their research shows that burnout is a common feature of correctional officer life. Sixty-four percent of the COs they examined reported moderate or high levels of emotional exhaustion as a result of their work. Moderate or high levels of depersonalization were reported by 80% of the officers, while similar levels of a lack of personal accomplishment were experienced by 82% of the officers under study.

Utilizing an earlier version of the same measure, Whitehead and Lindquist (1986) probed the causes of burnout among 220 correctional officers employed by the Alabama Department of Corrections. Emotional exhaustion was found to be the direct result of stress, feelings of role conflict, and a lack of administrative support. Both a lack of job satisfaction and an officer's age were indirectly related to emotional exhaustion. The relationship of age to emotional exhaustion was similar to the previously discussed relationship between age and stress. Older officers appeared to suffer from lower levels of emotional exhaustion than their younger co-workers. This was most likely the result of older officers having developed better coping skills as their life experience has increased. The problem of depersonalization was determined to be the direct result of an officer's age (being younger), a lack of administrative support, and feelings of role conflict. Other variables contributed very little to depersonalization. The third component of burnout, a lack of personal accomplishment, appeared to be the direct result of three variables. Both a lack of job satisfaction and a lack of participation in decision making were both important in causing correctional officers to experience a lack of personal accomplishment in their work. Interestingly, the third variable, the amount of inmate contact experienced by a CO, was related to a lack of personal accomplishment but in the opposite direction than was predicted. Higher amounts of inmate contact resulted in higher levels of perceived personal accomplishment, whereas traditional thinking about burnout would assume the opposite to be true. The authors theorized that in the case of correctional officers most contact with inmates is superficial, not involving the time and depth of interaction that other human service workers generally experience in the course of their work with clients.

Similar findings concerning the causality of burnout were found among correctional officers in Arizona (Merlak and Hepburn, 1992). Stress was found to cause burnout, and again, older COs appeared to be shielded from its effects. As in the case of stress, burnout apparently is a cumulative process. These authors observed that correctional officers who had worked in prison for longer periods of time suffered from higher levels of burnout than did their junior colleagues.

Alienation

Another social psychological malady that has been found to beset correctional officers is alienation. Arguably the most influential discussion of alienation was advanced by Seeman (1959). Alienation, in Seeman's view, is a distinctly social psychological process in that it is defined by the subjective perceptions of the individual actor, not by any objective criteria defined by society. As a concept, Seeman sees alienation as incorporating five phenomena; powerlessness, meaninglessness, normlessness, isolation, and self-estrangement. Each interacts with the others to create the experience of alienation within the individual.

While most civilians would be quite surprised by the fact, correctional officers do suffer from subjective feelings of *powerlessness* within the prison environment. Although frequently depicted in the media as having total control over inmates, the reality of CO power in prisons is, as previously discussed in Chapter 4, very different. Seeman (1959: 784) observes that one common definition of powerlessness is "the expectancy or probability held by the individual that his own behavior cannot determine the occurrence of outcomes, or reinforcements, he seeks". Therefore powerlessness among correctional officers is broader than simply the problem of controlling inmates, although this of course is certainly an area where powerlessness does exist. But powerlessness can be experienced due to a lack of input into decision-making, a lack of opportunity to affect the overall goals of the institution, or even by the failure to bring about any meaningful change in the lives of the offenders with whom they work. Powerlessness appears to be endemic in jobs where the classical organizational pyramid and paramilitary organization sees employees as people to be controlled, rather than as worthwhile resources to be valued and utilized.

A second aspect of alienation is *meaninglessness*. This phenomenon is related to Durkheim's concept of "anomie", which is defined as "a situation in which the social norms regulating individual conduct have broken down or are no longer effective as rules for behavior" (Seeman, 1959: 787). Furthermore, the definition of meaninglessness is augmented by Merton's discussion of anomie, in which "there is a high expectancy that socially unapproved behaviors are required to achieve given goals" (Seeman, 1959: 788). Both of these situations can easily happen to a correctional officer during the course of his/her duties. Many COs were trained when security was the major aspect of the CO role. When the prevailing correctional philosophy changed to rehabilitation these officers found that the rules had changed and that their previous occupational behaviors were no longer acceptable. When the "correctional pendulum" swung again, this time away from rehabilitation, COs who were recruited and trained to aid in the rehabilitative process suddenly found it was their turn to find their definition of the CO role was no longer congruent with the expectations of correctional administrators. This form of normlessness may then contribute not only to alienation but also to a problem known as "role conflict", a process that will be discussed later in this chapter. In addition, many correctional officers find that the formally prescribed rules governing their behavior are simply not realistic, and that "informal" rules must be developed among COs in order for them to do their jobs. These informal rules may be at variance with the formal rules of the organization, and newer officers may be at a loss to understand which set of rules are operative at any given time. For example, many correctional officers feel the rules governing their ability to control inmates, developed by administrators and judges, are not reasonable. Unable to control inmates or protect themselves within these socially acceptable strictures, COs at times find it necessary to bend the rules, or even break them, in order to achieve the assigned goal of controlling inmates. While in these situations officers are operating outside official policy, or perhaps even in violation of statute, they see themselves as having no choice other than to do so. When COs are unable to determine the prescribed norms established to govern their behavior, or they realize the prescribed norms are completely irrelevant to their professional situation, meaninglessness in the workplace may result.

Isolation is the fourth variant of alienation identified by Seeman. While not used in the identical manner as the commonly used term "social isolation", Seeman (1959: 789) defines isolation as "assign(ing) low reward value to goals and beliefs that are typically highly valued in the given society". Using this definition it is difficult to decide if correctional officers are any more prone to isolation than are many other occupational groups in society. However, if one slightly expands this concept to "social isolation", as was done by Dean (1961) in his formulation of alienation, then one can more easily accept the idea that correctional officers may be isolated. Surely, being locked up in a total institution for eight hours a day, in an alien world characterized by a unique jargon, an anti-

94

social inmate subculture, and stereotyped by an ill-informed public that neither understands nor appreciates their efforts, might lead some officers to feel separated from society in general.

The final manner in which alienation has been conceptualized is as *self-estrangement*. Seeman (1959: 790) states that self-estrangement "refer(s) essentially to an inability of the individual to find self-rewarding.......activities that engage him". Thus individuals who suffer from self-estrangement derive little intrinsic reward from their work, but rather their work becomes simply a means by which they acquire extrinsic rewards. Correctional officers who experience self-estrangement would not come to work because they believed they were helping inmates change into better citizens, or they were making society a safer place to live because they were keeping predators under lock and key, or they were furthering the cause of justice by making criminals pay for their crimes. Rather, self-estranged COs come to work each day for one reason - their paycheck. Work has lost all meaning to them except as a mechanism by which they are able to pay the bills and feed their families. These officers do exist, and are discussed by Kauffman (1988) in her typology of correctional officers (see Chapter 6).

Alienation is a serious and complex phenomenon, and an awareness its causes is vital for developing an understanding the correctional officer's world. That COs suffer from alienation is clear. Research in several New York prisons revealed that seven out of every ten COs were alienated; one of four strongly so. Further, three of four felt the average officer would change jobs if he/she were able (Toch and Klofas, 1982).

Utilizing Seeman's conceptualization of alienation, both Poole and Regoli (1981) and Poole and Pogrebin (1987) examined several factors and that effected the occurrence of alienation among correctional officers. Specifically, these authors were interested in examining the effects of both interpersonal relationships and judicial intervention in the workplace to determine if they caused COs to become alienated. Powerlessness was found to be the result of officers having poor relationships with inmates and superiors, as well as feeling that the courts had gone too far in interfering with their role as a CO. Not having the ability to control inmates when they were unruly, and not being supported by the administration, contributed to a perception of workplace powerlessness. In addition, COs who felt that the courts had negatively impacted institutional discipline and control, along with providing inmates with too many legal protections, also suffered from high levels of powerlessness. Normlessness also was related to a perception of excessive judicial intervention, as were having poor relationships with both superiors and fellow officers. The courts were seen as changing the rules, and experiencing poor relationships with other officers left some COs without any source of understanding just how they were supposed to behave. Again, suffering from poor relationships with superiors appeared to cut them off from the only other avenue available for understanding their role within the institution. Meaninglessness appeared to be the result of poor relationships with inmates and again with a perception of needless judicial meddling. Correctional officers found it difficult to understand the purpose of their job when confronted by inmates who were abusive, unable or unwilling to change, and generally unappreciative of any assistance that the officers were unable to provide. Court decisions affecting institutional operations, which many time effected prison safety and provided inmates with benefits COs felt they did not deserve, added to feelings of meaninglessness. Correctional officers who suffered from isolation had poor relationships with inmates, the administration, and with fellow COs. This effectively cut them off from all social support networks within the institution. Again, those COs who perceived that the courts had become excessive in their intervention into prison operation felt increasingly isolated. Lastly, COs who experienced self-estrangement had poor relationships with fellow officers and perceived excessive judicial intervention into their work role. Finding no solidarity with their CO brethren, and feeling betrayed by the courts, these officers relied solely on extrinsic rewards to keep them on the job. Thus, all forms of alienation appear to result from both failed working relationships within the workplace and a perception that the courts have made it virtually impossible for correctional officers to do their job as they see it.

Other research underscores the problem of administrative action (or inaction) in the occurrence of alienation among COs. Toch and Klofas (1982) observed this same phenomenon, while noting that many alienated officers felt that inmates were treated better than they were by the prison administration, and that the administration appeared to care more about the inmates than it did about the welfare of the COs. Hepburn (1987) also observed that problems between COs, the administration, and inmates could lead to alienation. Officers perceived that they had less actual control in the prison than did either the inmates or the prison administration. This actual deficit in power, in addition to perceived differences in ideal levels of control between themselves and both the administration and inmates, led to increased levels of alienation among COs.

Personality characteristics and their relationship to alienation among correctional officers has also been examined. Mid-level supervisory COs who had a strong belief in self-regulation and a sense of "calling" to the field appeared to be shielded from alienation (Poole and Regoli, 1983). Among rank and file COs, a sense of calling to the field and a belief in individual autonomy characterized those officers who experienced lower levels of alienation (Poole and Regoli, 1980).

Several other variables were found to be significantly related to alienation. Younger correctional officers, those who had experienced what they defined as a "career turning point", those with longer service as COs, those who were assigned to lower security levels, and those who felt that the basic role of a CO was to provide prison security, all suffered from higher levels of alienation (Walters, 1991). As one custody-oriented, highly alienated officer remarked:

> "On my third day on the job I was called an asshole 20 times, a cocksucker 10 times, a motherfucker 13 times, and was told my mother fucked niggers 3 times. To sum up my attitude there are about 60 inmates I would kill given a legal opportunity, about 40 inmates I would go out of my way to help, *and the rest I plain don't care about at all* " (Walters, 1991: 57).

Role Conflict

While ensuring the security of a prison is always foremost in minds of correctional officers, their professional duties entail more that just locking cells. As discussed in Chapter One, Robert Johnson (1996) has defined two additional functions of correctional officers - providing human services, and aiding in the rehabilitative process. The "balance" between these three activities varies from prison to prison based on security level and prevailing correctional philosophy. Yet these three duties are always operative to some extent. Unfortunately these duties can, and do, often conflict with one another. For example, a CO one day may counsel an inmate about problems the inmate is experiencing adapting to the realities of prison life. Yet the following day the CO may be required to use physical force against the same inmate when the inmate refuses an order to change living areas. This problem has been commonly referred to as *role conflict*. Role conflict occurs when a individual's role entails actions that interfere or conflict with other actions the individual's role also requires. Individuals experiencing role conflict find that they are "damned if they do, damned if they don't", and simply don't know what their roles are within the institution. The evidence is clear that some correctional officers suffer from role conflict, and this conflict is related to other social psychological problems experienced by COs (Poole and Regoli, 1980: Hepburn and Albonetti, 1980).

Several causal factors have been identified which appear to effect the presence of role conflict among COs. Those correctional officers who have chosen their profession because they have a sense of calling to the field, and those who have a strong belief in self-regulation, appear to suffer less from role conflict than do other COs (Poole and Regoli, 1980, 1983). Correctional staff who work in minimum security institutions, including both COs and the treatment staff, also experience more role conflict than do those correctional personnel in other security level institutions. However, this increased role conflict was not thought to be caused by the positions themselves, but rather due to the institutional goals of minimum security institutions. These institutions, particularly those with an espoused treatment orientation, may be failing at their attempt to offer the "best of both worlds". Rather, treatment personnel feel that there is not enough emphasis on treatment while COs feel that there is not enough emphasis on security, causing both groups to suffer from role conflict in the workplace (Hepburn and Albonetti, 1980).

Cynicism

Given the psychological strains, conflicts with administration and inmates, and the conflicting demands placed upon correctional officers in modern correctional facilities, it is understandable that many COs become cynical about their occupational role. These officers develop feelings of animosity, antagonism, and disillusionment toward their work (Poole and Regoli, 1980). Cynicism is not equally distributed among the correctional officer corps. Rather, several factors, both structural and personal, have been identified as increasing the risk of becoming cynical. Farmer (1977) observed that most COs were cynical about their work, but those who were employed in a treatment-oriented institution were more cynical than their counterparts in other types of institutions. It was hypothesized that treatment-oriented institutions cause more role conflict among the COs, and thus cynicism became a survival defense mechanism developed by officers to cope with the conflicting demands placed upon them. Interpersonal relationships in the workplace and the amount of professionalism among COs has also been linked to cynicism (Poole and Regoli, 1980a; 1980b). In order of importance, poor relationships with superiors, other correctional officers, and inmates, can all lead to experiencing cynicism in the workplace. On the other hand, those COs who feel that they have a sense of calling to the field of corrections, and those who have a strong belief in self-regulation, seem to experience lower levels of cynicism than do other officers.

Job Satisfaction

The preceding discussions imply that correctional officers may well find their chosen career experience to be somewhat grim. And to be sure, there is a great deal of evidence to indicate that many correctional officers do not find their work to be very satisfying. While three out of four correctional officers report that their job is either "somewhat" or "very" satisfying, this number has been decreasing over the years, and it is lower than for most other occupational groups. Sixty percent of COs state that they would prefer another job, and almost one-half have had second thoughts about taking the job. Furthermore, most would not recommend the job of correctional officer to others (Cullen et al., 1989). Even when compared to other correctional employees, such as caseworkers and office staff, correctional officers exhibit lower levels of job satisfaction (Blau et al., 1986).

Demographically, COs who are satisfied with their jobs differ from their less satisfied brethren. Several authors have observed an inverse relationship between education and job satisfaction (Walters, 1993, 1996; Cullen et al., 1989; Jurik et al., 1987). Doubtless a disturbing finding for those interested in the professionalization of corrections, this relationship is not surprising. As has been previously noted, prisons are organized in a classical organization pyramid. This organizational form places most decision-making in the hand of administrators. Low ranking individuals within this type of organization are allowed little or no input, and are closely supervised by superiors. While a functional structure for controlling subordinates with little ability, this bureaucratic form can be stiffling for those educated officers who want to make a contribution to the operation of the prison.

Other demographic differences exist between satisfied and dissatisfied correctional officers. Minority COs appear to be less satisfied with correctional work than do white officers (Blau et al., 1986; Cullen et al., 1989). Some evidence also exists that female COs are more satisfied with their work than are male officers (Merlak and Hepburn, 1992). Finally, older COs exhibit higher levels of job satisfaction than do their junior co-workers (Blau et al., 1986).

Most research reveals that characteristics of the workplace are more important determinants of job satisfaction than are the individual demographic characteristics of correctional officers. As has been shown before, prison administrative practices can have a powerful effect on the social psychology of COs. Lombardo (1989) notes that dissatisfied correctional officers complain of a lack of responsibility and a lack of input into the decision-making process. They also perceive a lack of communication with the prison administration and a lack of support from it. Taken together, these administratively related problems contribute to feelings of "powerlessness" that decrease the amount of job satisfaction COs experience. Two correctional officers observed:

> "Here at the prison the Peter Principle is alive and doing well. It is almost impossible to get a decision out of management. Therefore it is impossible for me to do my job" (Walters, 1985).

> "Total lack of communication and if there is any it is usually negative. No moral support. The feeling is that we are dirt under their fingernails" (Walters, 1985).

Interaction with inmates can also have a powerful effect on an officer's job satisfaction. The physical danger that inmates may pose, and its related mental strain, decreases CO job satisfaction. So does the constant disrespectful treatment afforded correctional officers by some inmates, even while trying to treat them in a fair manner (Lombardo, 1989). Interestingly, Blau et al. (1986) observed the greater the number of inmate grievances filed against an officer, the more satisfied the officer was with his work. The authors hypothesized that this was the result of officer's working in security-oriented institutions where they were required to keep inmates under stricter social control. This interpretation is supported by Hepburn and Knepper (1993) who report that COs who perceive having authority over inmates also have greater job satisfaction. Yet maintaining a good attitude toward inmates does increase an officer's satisfaction with his/her work (Jurik et al., 1987).

An officer's job satisfaction is also effected by the work environment. Those COs who have good working relationships with their co-workers find increased satisfaction in their occupational role (Walters, 1993, 1996; Grossi and Berg, 1991; Jurik et al., 1987). Job satisfaction has been found to increase when correctional officers are able to engage in human service activities as a part of their job, thus alleviating some of the tedium that can accompany correctional work

(Hepburn and Knepper, 1993).

There are also interactions among the other social psychological pressures impinging upon correctional officers and their level of job satisfaction. High levels of stress reduce a COs job satisfaction (Walters, 1993, 1996; Blau et al., 1986). Further, both burnout and role conflict appear to decrease the amount of satisfaction a CO can derive from their employment (Hepburn and Knepper, 1993; Merlak and Hepburn, 1992).

Suicide

Tragically, in some cases the pressures resulting from correctional work may lead to suicide. Kamerman (1995) observes that there is more literature pertaining to inmate suicide than to suicide among correctional officers. Yet his research shows that the New York City Department of Correction correctional officers commit suicide at a rate similar to New York City Police officers. Unfortunately, this problem has been widely ignored. Kamerman gives several reasons for this fact. As we have already noted, correctional officers have a lower profile than police, and thus they are less understood by the public. In addition, policy makers themselves have shied away from addressing this problem.

Summary

Plainly the correctional institution, as a workplace, can be a psychologically hazardous environment. The research clearly shows that correctional officers do suffer, in varying degrees, from stress, burnout, alienation, role conflict, cynicism, and job dissatisfaction. Many of these processes interact with others in a "feedback loop", each augmenting the other. While the precise interaction pattern between these processes is unknown, Merlak and Hepburn (1992) have developed a path analysis model that is rather compelling . After looking at possible permutations, the authors feel that stress causes burnout, and that burnout in turn leads to a loss of job satisfaction.

One fact stands out in the analysis of all of these social psychological processes, and that is the importance of prison administrative practices in their causality. Correctional officers perceive real difficulties between themselves and those who manage correctional facilities. To help ameliorate this problem, several administrative innovations, generally collectively referred to as *participatory management*, have been suggested. Benton and Nesbitt (1988) suggest several ways in which the correctional workplace can be improved for COs. These authors suggest that employee incentive and motivational programs be implemented that reward COs for attaining clear and specified organizational goals. Furthermore, the job itself should be redesigned, allowing for job rotation, cross-training, the enhancement of employee autonomy and discretion, and employee input and feedback. This type of "job enlargement" has been found to be successful for correctional officers (Hepburn and Knepper, 1993; Toch and Klofas, 1982). The use of task forces to address special problems, quality circles, and joint labor-management committees are suggested for allowing more officer input into decision-making. Benton and Nesbitt also recommend that correctional managers be better trained in "people management", including trusting and respecting line officers, and better responding to the needs of COs. Mentoring programs are also encouraged, whereby newer officers are paired with compatible, more experienced volunteer COs who will assist the junior colleague better adapt to the problems encountered in prison work. Finally, employee assistance programs should be set in motion to aid COs in dealing with any psychological/emotional/physical problems that may result from an officer's workplace experiences. One very influential correctional innovation, *unit management*, has been very successful and incorporates many of the precepts of participatory management.

It would be unreasonable to expect that correctional officers should escape from their workplace psychologically unscathed. After all, they work in prisons. These institutions are the end result of a criminal justice system which systematically selects out the most anti-social and violent of offenders for incarceration in our overcrowded prisons. Working with inmates such as these will always be stressful and involve psychological risks. However, correctional officers expect difficulties with inmates - it's a part of the job. But they also expect to be supported in their endeavors by a prison administration that backs the officers' decisions, listens to their problems, and takes seriously their input concerning prison operations. The available research suggests that many COs would benefit from some administrative reform.

6

THE SUBCULTURE OF CORRECTIONAL OFFICERS

Criminologists have long been interested in how the various practitioners employed in the criminal justice system view their respective professional worlds. Most early research focused on police officers, as they are the most visible criminal justice agents to the citizenry. One early study done in the 1950's by Westley (1970) identified a police subculture characterized by secrecy, violence, and group solidarity. Police officers thought they could trust no one other than themselves, and violence was an acceptable means of maintaining the respect of citizens. Skolnick (1966) observed that police officers had a "working personality" that was comprised of two components. These components were danger and authority. Because of the danger of police work, police officers became suspicious of almost everyone with whom they interact. They utilized authority as a means to control others, and thus lessen the threat to themselves and their fellow officers.

Later criminologists developed typologies to identify different types of police officers. Broderick (1977) classified police officers into four categories based on two variables; a commitment to maintaining order, and a respect for due process. *Enforcers* were mainly concerned with order, and had little respect for

106

due process of law. *Idealists* were concerned with insuring that both social order and due process were achieved. *Optimists* were enamored with due process and had less concern with social order. Finally, *realists* had little faith in either the social order or in due process of law. A final typology of police officers by Muir (1977) is also of interest. Muir also noted four differing types of police officers. The *professional* had both "passion", defined as an understanding of human suffering, and "perspective", defined as an understanding that only legitimate means are acceptable in alleviating human suffering. The second type of officer, the *enforcer*, had the passion necessary for police work, but failed to have the requisite perspective for the job. *Reciprocators* had perspective but lacked passion, many times making them too detached from the human suffering which surrounded them. The last category, *avoiders*, possessed neither passion nor perspective, and thus failed to both recognize people's problems or take action to solve their difficulties.

Early analysis of correctional officers began by looking at some of the problems they faced on the job. Sykes (1958) observed correctional officers were often confronted by two opposing problems; the need to control inmates, and the need to satisfy administrators. This forced the COs into forming informal relationships with inmates, as the officers lacked the numbers and power to control inmates without their active assistance. By doing so they could gain the inmates' cooperation in maintaining the peace within the institution, which was the overriding concern of the prison administration.

Later research on the working world of correctional officers can be divided into three phases (Stojkovic, 1996). The first stage was concerned with examining individual CO demographic characteristics and their attitudes. The second stage moved away from an emphasis on individual officer demographics and entered into an examination of factors related to the prison organization itself. This research was interested in such phenomena as role conflict, custody orientation, job stress, and job satisfaction, to name a few. The final stage examined the concept of *subculture* as it applied to correctional officers. This work is quite interesting, and needs to be examined at length.

The Concept of Subculture

Hoult (1969: 322) maintains the term "subculture" has been used in three different ways:

> A) in some anthropological publications, denotes certain universals that are either part of all societies or constitute an aspect of the foundations of all cultures; B) the normative system of a group smaller than a total society (i.e. an ethnic enclave such as French Canadians in New England, or even a relatively temporary group such as a friendship circle), a phenomenon T. Lasswell has labeled a *microculture*; and C) the normative system of a sub-group whose members are subjected to such systemic frustration that they develop values which are almost consciously contrary to those prevailing in the larger society (i.e., the values of a lower class juvenile gang), a usage that has prompted introduction of a new concept, *contraculture*.

While an exact definition of the term is lacking in some relevant research, it is the second definition that appears to be the operative concept in most of the literature on the working world of correctional officers.

By looking at previous research on police subcultures, and carefully examining the social environment of prisons, several factors can be linked to the development of a correctional officer subculture. One important factor is *conflict*. Correctional officers are in conflict with two groups. The first, and most obvious, are the inmates (Walters, 1986). COs must gain the compliance of inmates to their directives, and many times inmates are not enthusiastic in complying. Verbal abuse from inmates is a common occurrence. Officers are sometimes the targets of feces and urine thrown by inmates. And of course there is the possibility of physical violence, ranging from punches, kicks, and bites to choking and stabbing. The second source of conflict is the prison administration (Jacobs, 1978; Webb and Morris, 1978; Kinsell and Sheldon, 1981; Walters, 1986; Lombardo, 1988). Officers commonly feel the prison administration fails to support them in their efforts. These sentiments are reflected in the words of correctional officers from a prison in the western U.S.:

> "Every day is a turning point. If you're not stabbed in the back by an inmate, the administration will do it" (Walters, 1991: 55).

> "In this prison you've got to watch your back from both the inmates and the administration" (Walters, 1991: 55).

> "COs I've worked with have been beaten and stabbed just to be told to 'hit the road, Jack.' You can be replaced rather than allowed to come back. As soon as you are injured they don't want you back, you're a liability. This administration shows absolutely no regard for staff. 'If you don't like it here go somewhere else, we have 500 applicants wanting your job'" (Walters, 1986: 92).

Indeed, Jacobs and Retsky (1980: 181) go so far as to state:

> ....it would not be an exaggeration to say that administrators and treatment personnel feel more respect and a greater affinity for the inmate than they do for the guard.

Thus, COs are forced to band together into a cohesive group in order to survive in an environment they perceive as hostile.

The concept of *danger*, previously alluded to, also helps foster the development of a correctional officers subculture. In most prisons officers are greatly outnumbered by inmates, and the possibility of physical injury, or even death, always looms in the back of many COs minds. The only security officers on the prison floors have is one another. Each individual officer knows the only person that will be there when they are in peril are their fellow correctional officers. This mutual interdependence greatly helps facilitate subcultural formation.

Another factor which may contribute to the formation of a correctional officer subculture is *isolation*. The isolation experienced by COs is both physical and social. The physical isolation of prisons is, or course, intentional. Commonly located in rural areas, prisons are surrounded by either high walls, a variety of perimeter security technologies, or both. This perimeter security has two functions; to keep inmates in, and to keep civilians out. Unlike police officers, who conduct most of their duties in public, the world of the correctional officer is a mystery to most civilians. The image of a CO to most civilians is what they see in the media, an image which is false and degrading to most officers (Berger, 1978; Walters, 1986; Walters, 1988). The prison administration also increases this social isolation by many times discouraging COs from discussing happenings within the institution with outsiders, particularly the media. Correctional officers also add to the problem, as a common saying among many COs is "what happens behind the walls, stays behind the walls". Misunderstood by the public, and segregated behind prison walls, COs can easily become so isolated from the world in general they feel no one else either understands them or supports them in their efforts to protect society.

Correctional officers generally also share some similar *background characteristics* that may contribute to the evolution of a CO subculture. Most prisons are located in rural areas, and many times recruit officers from these areas. This insures that many officers will hold rural attitudes and values in common. Even when the prison locale differs from the norm, Carroll (1988) observed that correctional officers are solidly middle-class in their lifestyle and

110

ideology. This separates them from the inmate subculture, which is predominately urban and lower-class in origin. Thus these background similarities both bind officers together and serve to differentiate them from others in the prison environment.

Characteristics of the Correctional Officer Subculture

Correctional officers are not born with a knowledge of the CO subculture. Rather, it is learned through interaction with other officers, inmates, and the prison administration. This process, termed *prisonization* by Clemmer (1958), refers to the process by which inmates, and COs, learn the norms, values, language, and behaviors that permeate the prison world. Some characteristics of the CO subculture can be found in the official rules and regulations of the prison. These "formal norms" aid the officer in understanding the prison world. However, most are a part of the "informal norms" of prison life. These informal norms many times differ from the formal norms of the prison, and in some cases mandate behaviors that are in direct opposition to the proscribed formal norms.

Subcultures are characterized by the existence of identifiable elements. One of these elements is a specialized language, or *argot*, spoken by the members of the subculture. Sykes (1958) detailed the inmate argot at a New Jersey prison. Correctional officers must learn this inmate language is they are to survive in the prison environment. Not only do COs utilize the inmate argot, but there are specialized terms of their own that they use in their day-to-day duties. Terms such as "shakedown", "sallyport", and "shank" are either undecipherable or used in a different manner than they are by society in general.

Correctional officers must also learn the proper *attitudes* toward other officers, inmates, and the administration. Should inmates be trusted? Should fellow COs be trusted? Do inmate's ever change? Is it appropriate to "shade" a written report? Is it important to follow the written rules, or are there times and situations where it is acceptable to violate them? These attitudes are all learned from an officer's experiences working in the prison and from his/her interaction with other COs.

Learning prescribed *behaviors* is an essential part of becoming socialized into the correctional officers subculture. Officers must know what their colleagues expect them to do, and they must know what types of behaviors are proscribed. Some of these behaviors are "by the book" activities that are desired by officers and the administration alike. Other times, however, prescribed subcultural behaviors may be diametrically opposed to the administration's desires.

The subculture of correctional officers can be better understood by examining what has been called the "correctional officer code" (Kauffman, 1988; Farkas, 1997). Theoretically similar to the often-discussed "inmate code" (Sykes and Messenger, 1960), this code is an unwritten set of shared assumptions about how COs should act on the job. Violating the code can bring about sanctions from fellow officers ranging from mild rebukes to virtual social ostracism.

Kelsey Kauffman's (1988) book *Prison Officers and Their World* contains the first truly comprehensive discussion of the correctional officer code. Her analysis identified nine norms of behavior which constituted the CO code at four state prisons for men in Massachusetts. First and foremost among these norms is *always go to the aid of an officer in distress.* This norm is paramount for correctional officers. Most COs work alone, and they are always vastly outnumbered by the inmates in their charge. Alone and unarmed, the only recourse an officer has when attacked is to call for the assistance of fellow officers. These officers must react quickly, effectively, and without hesitation. It is imperative for a CO come to the assistance for two reasons. First, failure to respond could result in serious injury or even death for another officer. Second, a CO never knows when he/she will be the victim of an attack. Thus responding quickly when another officer is attacked serves as a type of "insurance policy" for an officer. Violating this norm by failing to assist another officer in distress may well lower the probability that others will assist you when you are in peril.

FIGURE 6.1
INFORMAL CORRECTIONAL OFFICER CODE

Kauffman (1988)

•Always go to the aid of an officer in distress.
•Don't "lug" drugs.
•Don't rat.
•Never make a fellow officer look bad in front of inmates.
•Always support an officer in a dispute with an inmate.
•Always support officer sanctions against inmates.
•Don't be a "white hat".
•Maintain officer solidarity versus all outside groups.
•Show positive concern for fellow officers.

Farkas (1997)

•Always go to the aid of an officer in real or perceived physical danger.
•Don't get too friendly with inmates.
•Don't abuse your authority with inmates. Keep your cool.
•Back your fellow officers in decisions and actions; don't stab a co-worker in the back.
•Cover your ass and do not admit mistakes.
•Carry your own weight.
•Defer to the experience and wisdom of veteran COs.
•Mind your own business.

The subcultural norm *don't lug drugs* is reflective of the disruptive affect that drugs have on the functioning of a prison. Unlike alcohol, which can be produced within the prison itself, drugs must be imported into the prison. Most are imported by prison employees, and sometimes even by correctional officers themselves. While most COs disapproved of drugs, it was not this disapproval that motivated the norm. Rather, it was the fear that inmates, whether under the influence of drugs or alcohol, could become aggressive and more violent after substance abuse. In other prisons inmate gangs have used drugs as the major form of contraband to gain and maintain power within the institution. While some officers smuggled drugs into the institution for money, Kauffman notes some COs violate this norm simply to buy themselves some peace with the inmates. Thus, the fear of violence from inmates was the motivating factor for some officers.

Kauffman's (1988) analysis lists *don't rat* as the third norm of the correctional officer subculture. The phrase refers to being an informant, in this case informing on fellow officers to either the prison administration or to the inmates. This is somewhat ironic as this same proscription has also been identified as an important part of the "inmate code" (Sykes and Messenger, 1960). Informing to inmates was considered a major breach of CO solidarity if it was a continual practice. Inmates many time do not know which officer filed a disciplinary report about them, or which officers may have been involved in quelling a disturbance that involved utilizing physical force. Providing inmates with information about fellow officers could place these officers in jeopardy of physical harm. Officers are also proscribed from providing information to the administration about the performance of their colleagues. Many COs, as previously discussed, do not feel their supervisors have their best interests at heart. Often officers believe the rules they are forced to work under are inadequate to control the prison and protect the safety of the COs. Therefore they occasionally must violate the official operating procedures of the prison, actions that could bring about a reprimand, suspension, or even dismissal. It is therefore thought imperative that these activities be shielded from the eyes of the administration.

Never make a fellow officer look bad in front of inmates was another element of the correctional officer code. Kauffman observed that even if a CO feels another CO has done something incorrect, it should never be pointed out in front of an inmate. The appearance of solidarity among the officers is very important, as they are always outnumbered by the inmates. "Putting down" a fellow officer in front of an inmate might allow the inmates to use this conflict as a wedge between officers. Differences between officers should always be handled away from inmate observers. Part of the motivation for this norm is the idea of reciprocity; most officers would not want to be criticized in front of an inmate, therefore they refused to do the same to another CO.

Kauffman identified *always support an officer in a dispute with an inmate* as another norm COs are expected to follow. The reasoning for this norm is similar to that of the previous norm. Correctional officer solidarity is an essential survival technique in prison environments where inmates consistently outnumber the officers. Kauffman states most COs consider inmates to be in the wrong, if not this time, then on previous occasions. Even if a CO is wrong, it is expected other COs will support that officer. Most COs want to be supported when they have a dispute with an inmate, therefore they feel a certain obligation to support their fellow COs.

In a related vein, *always support officer sanctions against inmates* is a logical corollary to the two previous norms of the CO subculture. Yet this norm goes beyond the simple enforcement of rules and regulations. Kauffman relates officers sometimes utilized coercion and physical violence as a means of social control. These acts were generally retaliatory in nature and were used as a means of deterring inmate violence. Still, many times these activities were a direct violation of the formal prison rules, but many COs still felt an obligation to participate in some way.

Don't be a white hat is yet another norm of the correctional officer subculture identified by Kauffman. A "white hat" is an officer who appears to have more sympathy for inmates than for fellow officers. These officers become too friendly with inmates, thus failing to maintain what is considered to be the proper social distance necessary to maintain CO solidarity. Officers who "act like an inmate" or "act like a social worker" are thought to make the job more difficult for the other officers who failed to be as accommodating with inmates.

While maintaining solidarity against inmates has been a common theme in the CO subculture, the norm *maintain officer solidarity versus all outside groups* takes this notion one step further. The distrust between COs and the prison administration has already been alluded to. Yet this norm extends beyond the prison walls. Other proscribed groups include the general public and the news media. Correctional officers are sensitive to the stereotypes that have been constructed about them, and they believe no one else really understands what they do or why they do it. The easiest way for the officers to deal with this problem is to simply shut out all outside groups from their social world.

Kauffman's final norm is *show positive concern for fellow officers.* This subculture norm is operative both on and off the job. On the job an officer was expected to never leave a problem on his/her shift to be dealt with by officers on later shifts. Fair play was considered to be the appropriate attitude at work. After work, COs commonly would help one another if serious problems, such as illness or injury, were to befall a fellow officer.

In a later study Farkas (1997) examined the correctional officer code in two prisons in the midwest. Several of the norms of behavior in each study are quite similar, lending credibility to both the quality of the research and the validity of the concept under study. However, four additional norms were observed by Farkas. *Don't abuse your authority with inmates. Keep your cool* is a norm of the CO subculture. Officers thought it inappropriate to harass inmates with no cause. This type of behavior only served to make the inmates more disgruntled and more likely to file complaints against officers. It not only increased the probability inmates might react violently, but might also trigger increased supervision from the administration. These consequences are undesirable and the causal behavior unnecessary, thus the proscriptive subcultural norm.

Cover your ass and do not admit to mistakes is an additional element of the correctional officer code identified by Farkas. This is another self-protective norm. Officers felt that if they admit to a mistake the administration will come to believe that all officers are acting in a similar manner, thus increasing the level of supervision for all.

Defer to the experience and wisdom of veteran COs is also part of the correctional officer code in Farkas' two midwestern prisons. Much of prison work can be highly subjective. While training is important, there is much about handling inmates that can only be learned through experience. Newer officers who thought they "knew it all" were disparaged by more senior officers who had more extensive personal knowledge of inmates and prison life.

Farkas (1997: 33-34) relates that the normative code of correctional officers is an extremely utilitarian phenomenon that provides a number of functions for the officers.

> First, it engenders a feeling of solidarity and brotherhood. Officers feel united in their decisions and course of action. Second, the "code" provides clarification of behavior for officers. Correctional officers form common modes of action from this knowledge of the boundaries of acceptable and prohibited behavior. It is a regulator of behavior, curbing and controlling certain forms, such as abuse or

collusion with inmates. Third, it provides a means of modifying or rejecting the formally proscribed modes of action and developing alternative strategies........ Fourth, the normative code teaches officers when to reveal or conceal information to management and outsiders. Officers are taught to "cover their asses" and not to admit mistakes. This provides officers with protection from managerial scrutiny, as well as from sanctions for their behavior. Fifth, the code allows officers to make supportive and meaningfully helpful relationships based on a commonality of action and values.

While the previous discussion of the officer code of behavior is interesting and useful, there are some criminologists who question whether a correctional officer subculture truly exists, or if it does, what form it may take. In an earlier work Kauffman (1981) observed correctional officers were characterized by "pluralistic ignorance". This phenomenon refers to a process where members of a group, such as COs, systematically misgauge the attitudes and values of other members of their group. In a study of nine correctional facilities in Connecticut, Kauffman (1981) found correctional officers consistently overestimated the number of anti-inmate COs while underestimating the number of COs who were more sympathetic toward inmates and treatment programs. Most officers assumed other COs held attitudes about inmates that were similar to their own. Curiously, correctional officers who held decidedly unsympathetic attitudes toward inmates were much more likely to feel their view was the dominant CO view than were officers who held more sympathetic attitudes. Anti-inmate attitudes were found to be less common than most COs realized, while attitudes sympathetic toward inmates were more frequent than commonly supposed. Thus the correctional officer subculture appears more pluralistic and diverse than outside observers, and COs themselves, might suppose.

Typologies of Correctional Officers

This "pluralistic ignorance" among correctional officers concerning their subculture was further examined by Klofas and Toch (1982) in four New York maximum security prisons. These authors developed one of the first typologies of correctional officers. A *typology* has been defined as "the intersection of two or more variables, therefore creating a set of categories or types" (Babbie, 1999: 166). By examining both a COs own attitude toward work, and a COs perception of fellow officers' attitudes toward work, these Klofas and Toch (1982) were able to develop a typology of correctional officers within the CO subculture.

The first subgroup of correctional officers, the *discouraged subculturalists*, were officers who held attitudes Klofas and Toch termed "not professional", but assumed other officers held "professional" attitudes. Non-professional attitudes are defined as pro-custodial, alienated, and anti-inmate. On the other hand, a professional attitude is defined as more progressive, interested in treatment, and more understanding of inmates and their problems. What is extremely interesting about this CO subgroup is that it is merely theoretical. Klofas and Toch (1982) were unable to find any officers that fit this category. This is interesting in that officers who possessed attitudes that the authors define as not professional all assumed that all other COs share their attitudes. These officers could not fathom that there were correctional officers whose attitudes concerning correctional work would be defined as professional by the authors, even though most officers do in fact hold these attitudes.

The *subcultural custodians* were correctional officers who held non-professional attitudes and assumed other COs shared their same values. While these officers appeared to fit the stereotype of correctional officers, they were in fact the smallest of the CO subgroups. However, they could be very vocal in their viewpoint and may influence other officer subgroups. They were also most likely to be found among those officers with the least amount of experience as correctional officers. Figure 6.2 details this typology.

FIGURE 6.2
KLOFAS AND TOCH CORRECTIONAL OFFICER TYPOLOGY

See Self as....   *See Others as....*

	PROFESSIONAL	*NOT PROFESSIONAL*
NOT PROFESSIONAL	**Discouraged Subculturalists** n = 0 0% of total 0% of pure types	**Subcultural Custodians** n = 130 17% of total 21.8% of pure types
PROFESSIONAL	**Supported Majority** n = 265 34.7% of total 44.5% of pure types	**Lonely Braves** n = 200 26.2% of total 33.6% of pure types

Source: Klofas, John and Toch, Hans. (1982). "The Guard Subculture Myth". *Journal of Research in Crime and Delinquency* 19: p 247.

Contrary to the commonly held image of correctional officers, the largest subgroup of correctional officers were the *supported majority*. Members of this subgroup held professional attitudes and felt other COs shared their same attitudes and values. These officers comprised almost 45% of the COs who fit into one of the typology categories. The supported majority was not anti-inmate, was not alienated, and saw their professional role as being more than simply providing a security function. These officers generally were those who had the greatest amount of experience as a CO.

The final sub-group identified by Klofas and Toch (1982) were the *lonely braves*. These correctional officers perceived themselves as holding professional attitudes but felt other COs did not share their perspective. As in all other cases, except for the support majority, these officers displayed pluralistic ignorance in that they assumed their co-workers did not share their professional attitudes when in fact the majority did.

A second typology of correctional officers was developed by Kauffman (1988) in four Massachusetts prisons (see Figure 6.3). The interrelationship between two variables were utilized to categorize officers in this typology; an officer's attitude toward inmates, and an officer's attitude toward their fellow officers.

In examining the relationship between an officer's attitudes toward inmates and officers, Kauffman identified five types of correctional officers operating within the prisons she studied. Theoretically, this typology could have predicted nine possible subcultures, however, only five were found that actually represented the attitudes of correctional officers.

Kauffman (1988) identified *pollyannas* as correctional officers who held positive attitudes toward both inmates and their fellow officers. This attempt at living in both worlds was a very difficult endeavor. In the polarized prison world correctional officers who were identified as pollyannas were distrusted by both inmates and other officers. Most pollyannas held their peers in high personal regard, even when they disagreed with their personal tactics in dealing with inmates or with the prison rules themselves. Commonly they felt sorry for inmates and took great personal satisfaction in being able to do even small things that bettered the life of their charges. The main way they were able to identify with both groups was by focusing on the individual, rather than stereotyping people into any particular category. This role was very difficult to maintain, thus Kauffman was able to identify only a very small number of them within the prison. All left prison work.

White Hats were correctional officers who held positive attitudes toward inmates but who did not hold their fellow officers in high esteem. As noted in the earlier discussion of the "correctional officer code", this type of officer was not accepted by other officers and in fact was respected less in than were pollyannas. Therefore it is not surprising that white hats comprised a relatively small number of COs. These officers shared a desire to make the lives of inmates a little better, and all seemed to genuinely enjoy the company of inmates. Most, but not all, of the white hats identified by Kauffman were college graduates who had hoped to change the correctional system from within. Many felt their fellow COs were too interested in authority, or were incompetent and indifferent in doing their jobs. Most of these officers also left prison work, either by being forced out by other officers or by simply resigning.

Officers almost diametrically opposed to white hats were a group Kauffman (1988) designated as *hard asses*. This group of correctional officers had no use for inmates whatsoever, and strongly identified with one another. Generally this subgroup of officers was younger and less experienced than most COs. They often reveled in the conflicts that characterized prison life, seeing their job as an adventure to be experienced. To them, prison life was a constant battle between good and evil, and they were the good guys. Regardless of the stereotype of correctional officers, these officers were relatively few in number. This seems reasonable, as being constantly at war with inmates takes a great deal of physical and psychological energy and puts an officer at risk of retaliation from inmates. Most of these officers eventually wearied of this role and either became "burnouts" or resigned.

FIGURE 6.3
KAUFFMAN CORRECTIONAL OFFICER TYPOLOGY

*attitude toward
inmates*   *attitude toward officers*

	POSITIVE	AMBIVALENT	NEGATIVE
POSITIVE	Pollyannas		White Hats
AMBIVALENT		Functionaries	
NEGATIVE	Hard Asses		Burnouts

Source: Kauffman, Kelsey. (1988). *Prison Officers and Their World.* Cambridge, MA: Harvard University Press, p. 249.

Burnouts were correctional officers who suffered from extreme emotional exhaustion. They found companionship with neither other officers nor inmates and therefore were isolated in the prison environment. Kauffman noted these COs are not only burned out as officers, "they are burned out as people" (Kauffman, 1988: 255). Their psychological distress not only existed inside of the prison, but it permeated their whole life. Prison stress evidenced itself in a paranoia where officers reacted to the entire world in the same way that they responded to prison life. Unfortunately, burnouts comprised a large number of COs in Kauffman study, perhaps being the majority of officers in one institution.

The final, and perhaps most unique subgroup of officers, were categorized by Kauffman as *functionaries*. These COs simply adapted to the prison world and its pressures by shutting themselves off psychologically from their environment. These officers didn't dislike their fellow officers or the inmates, but they cared very little for them one way or another. "Ambivalence" best describes their feeling for those around them in the workplace. They had no illusions about making the world a better place, or of being able to help offenders straighten out their lives. To these individuals being a correctional officer was a job, just like any other job. They were there to earn a paycheck, not for any type of emotional satisfaction. Their goal was survival.

Kauffman (1988: 260) observed very few officers came into prison work as a member of one subgroup and remained constant in that approach over the entire span of their correctional careers.

> More commonly, men in this study started out as Pollyannas, White Hats, or Hard Asses (in approximately that order of frequency), became Burnouts (some Pollyannas and White Hats became Hard Asses on their way to becoming Burnouts), following which they settled into the role of Functionary or resigned. Generally speaking, movement was from positive attitudes toward inmates and/or officers, to negative attitudes (first toward inmates, then toward officers), to physical or emotional withdrawal from the prison and everyone in it.

Summary

The research shows that correctional officers do indeed labor in a unique occupational world. These individuals are subjected to pressures, situations, and issues that few who work outside of the prison environment will ever be able to truly understand. Not all adapt in the same manner, but they all must learn to cope in one way or another with a common set of occupational circumstances and experiences.

Do correctional officers constitute a true "subculture"? Criminologists vary in degree to their answer to that question. Klofas and Toch (1982) felt generally the answer is "no". They saw too much variability in CO attitudes for a true subculture to exist, although they did believe that in some prisons the "stereotypical" procustodial subculture does exist while in others a majority of COs have a professional orientation. While this professional orientation doesn't fit the stereotype of the CO subculture, it may simply be the stereotype is, as many stereotypes are, simply wrong.

Klofas (1984) reiterated the "no" response, feeling correctional officers' attitudes are neither homogeneous enough or different enough for other occupational groups to warrant categorization as a subculture. The research certainly has shown that officers hold differing attitudes. But Klofas too used the procustodial stereotype of COs as a model when he stated correctional officers have not produced a subculture. Perhaps this stereotype needs to be abandoned.

A final thought on this issue was provided by Lombardo (1985: 85-86). While Lombardo also felt correctional officers do not fit the definition of a subculture most of the time, this can indeed change.

> However, under conditions of stress of "external danger" created by threats to the *status quo*, the subcultural values and group solidarity around these anti-inmate and anti-administration values are capable of mobilization. Guards emerge as a group in response to threats from the outside, while they act as isolated individuals under normal circumstances.

So does a correctional officer subculture exist? If the definition of the CO subculture assumes the stereotype that officers must be anti-inmate, unprofessional, and highly alienated from their jobs, then the answer is, of course, "no". If one defines a subculture as a monolithic belief system in which all members of the group completely believe, then the answer is again is generally "no", although one may find prisons where this is in fact the case. The research clearly states that in most institutional environments correctional officers hold a variety of attitudes and values about their profession. Correctional officers are required by their occupation to deal with issues concerning the basic nature of people, danger, isolation, and stress few other groups in society are forced to deal with. This may make COs a group sufficiently distinct to be conceptualized as a subculture. While not all COs make the identical decisions in dealing with these issues, face them they must. Perhaps one might discuss CO *subcultures* rather than a CO *subculture.* All in all, whether correctional officers comprise a distinct subculture may simply be a matter of semantics and of degree.

7

MINORITIES AS CORRECTIONAL OFFICERS

Considerable interest has been shown in broadening the gender and racial composition of the correctional officer corps. The employment of both women and African Americans as correctional officers has been seen as desirable for practical and legal reasons. Yet the integration of these groups into correctional employment has, historically speaking, been very different. Blacks have a long history of being employed as correctional officers in male prisons. Women, however, did not make their appearance as correctional officers in male prisons until the 1970's. Legal changes, along with some perceived behavioral characteristics, were the main motivation for employing women as COs. The interest in black COs was motivated by different factors. The overrepresentation of blacks in the prisons of America contrasted sharply with a CO force which was overwhelmingly white. Utilizing more African Americans as correctional officers was therefore thought to be an constructive change, and perhaps a means for lessening some of the racial violence that has come to characterize many American prisons. Yet while many justifications for employing both minorities may appear reasonable, the hard evidence needs to explored. It is possible that the rationales for utilizing these groups as officers in prisons were based more on

128

stereotypes than on reality. Are there any important differences between male officers and female officers? Do black correctional officers react to inmates any differently than their white CO colleagues? Or, is it possible the prison environment itself is more important in shaping correctional officer behavior than any individual characteristics COs may possess? Simple justice, and the law, demand equal employment opportunities for both groups. Yet both the rationales for the increased employment of minorities, and the empirical evidence as to their performance as correctional officers, needs to be explored if intelligent decisions are to be made regarding the staffing of American prisons.

WOMEN CORRECTIONAL OFFICERS

Women have played an important role in the evolution of modern correctional practices. Early reformers, such as Elizabeth Gurney Fry and Eliza Farnham, were responsible for numerous progressive innovations which resulted in more humane conditions for female inmates (Champion, 1990; Morris and Rothman, 1995). Individuals such as these were responsible for ending such practices as having female inmates supervised by male officers, thus alleviating the attending abuses that sometimes resulted. Under their auspices separate institutions for women were established, and programs attempting to rehabilitate and reform inmates were instituted.

Still, women were generally absent in correctional administration and are seldom seen in institutions housing male offenders. For the most part, women correctional officers, or *matrons* in the lexicon of the day, were restricted to duties involving the supervision of female offenders. Lekkerkerker (1931) relates that these matrons worked long hours for low pay, generally living at the prison in which they worked. They were expected to be role models and assist in the reformation of their female charges. This they generally did well until the 1930's, when the increased utilization of specialists in such fields as counseling and education, relegated matrons to the more limited role of providing security within the institution.

The Controversy Over Employing Women Officers in Male Prisons

This state of affairs continued until the 1970's, when women correctional officers were first regularly assigned to prisons housing male offenders. While at first their duties were confined to searching female visitors and administrative tasks, they soon were engaged almost all of the traditional CO duties (Pollack, 1986). There were several reasons offered for the sexual integration of the correctional officer staff in male prisons. Starting in the mid 1960's, and continuing through the 1970's, several legal changes occurred which aided women in their attempts to find employment as correctional officers in male institutions. Title VII of the 1964 Civil Rights Act, and several later federal court decisions, removed most of the legal barriers that had kept women from this type of employment (Zimmer, 1986; Jacobs, 1981; Peterson, 1982; Parisi, 1984). The rare court decision that appeared to hinder the employment of women, *Dothard v. Rawlinson*, 433 U.S. 321 (1977), was interpreted narrowly had only marginal affect on the increasing number of women becoming employed as COs in male prisons (Jacobs, 1981; Pollock-Byrne, 1990).

In addition to the legal pressure to employ women officers in male prisons, others hypothesized women would have a "normalizing" affect on prison life, making it more reflective of the multisexual world outside the prison walls (Morris and Hawkins, 1970; Peterson, 1982;). The presence of women would soften the hard, male-only world of the prison, and hopefully cause the

130

inmates to act in a more "civilized" manner. Furthermore, it was thought that women, who statistically appear less likely to act in an aggressive and violent manner, would utilize their superior verbal skills to defuse potentially violent confrontations with male inmates without resorting to coercive force (Kissel and Katsampes, 1980; Zimmer, 1986; Wicks, 1980). Those who favored a rehabilitative or reintegrative approach to corrections also advocated the assignment of women correctional officers to prisons housing male offenders. The perhaps stereotypical "feminine" image of women was thought to make women COs more accepting of a rehabilitative or social service role for correctional officers, thus increasing the probability of behavioral change in the inmates (Jurik, 1985; Crouch, 1985). The employment of women as correctional

FIGURE 7.1
AMERICAN CORRECTIONAL ASSOCIATION
POLICY ON EMPLOYMENT OF WOMEN IN CORRECTIONS

Introduction:

The American Correctional Association has a long-standing commitment to equal employment opportunity for women in adult and juvenile corrections.

Statement:

Women have a right to equal employment. No person who is qualified for a particular position/assignment or job-related opportunities should be denied such employment or opportunities because of gender. Therefore, correctional agencies should:

A. Ensure that recruitment, selection, and promotion opportunities are open to women;

B. Assign female employees duties and responsibilities that provide career development and promotional opportunities equivalent to those provided other employees;

C. Provide all levels of staff with appropriate training on developing effective and cooperative working relationships between male and female correctional personnel; and

D. Conduct regular monitoring and evaluation of affirmative action practices and take any needed corrective actions.

Source: Allen, Harry and Simonsen, Clifford. (1995). *Corrections in America.* Upper Saddle River, NJ: Prentice Hall, p. 685.

officers is seen as so beneficial that the American Correctional Association has championed their cause (see Figure 7.1).

Regardless of motivation, the numbers of women COs in American prisons increased steadily in the last three decades of the twentieth century. In 1973 women comprised 9.2% of all correctional officers (Chapman et al., 1983). By 1985 this number had increased to 12% (American Correctional Association, 1986), and by 1995 women comprised 19% of the CO force (U.S. Department of Justice, 1997). Not only had the numbers women increased rapidly, but their utilization in male prisons also increased from 6.6% of all COs in 1978 to 12.9% in 1988 (Morton, 1991).

TABLE 7.1
GENDER DISTRIBUTION OF CORRECTIONAL OFFICERS
IN AMERICAN PRISONS 1985 - 2002

	1985*	1990*	1995**	2000**	2002**
Total	92,955	168,972	213,370	254,871	255,860
Male	87.9%	83.4%	82.0%	77.9%	77.3%
Female	12.1%	16.6%	18.0%	22.1%	22.7%

*Source: Compiled by the author from U.S. Department of Justice, Bureau of Justice Statistics, *Sourcebook of Criminal Justice Statistics - 1988, 1989, 1990, 1991, 1992, 1993, 1994, 1998.* Washington, DC: U.S. Department of Justice.

**Source: Camp, C. (2003). *Corrections Yearbook 2002.* Middletown, CT: Criminal Justice Institute.

Although the increasing numbers of women working as correctional officers is impressive, it has not always been without resistance. A significant amount of research has shown that many male correctional officers received female officers in the workplace with something less than total acceptance (Peterson, 1982; Zimmer, 1986; Jurik, 1985; Owen, 1985; Horne, 1985; Walters,

1993). Those male officers who have resisted the entry of women into the prison environment have based their opposition on several concerns.

Several researchers (Jurik, 1985; Parisi, 1984; Simpson and White, 1985) have observed many male correctional officers feel women do not have the physical strength to deal with aggressive male inmates. Working in a prison constantly places one in potential physical danger. Inmates often assault other inmates and occasionally assault staff. Simple everyday activities, such as cell transfers, can escalate into an extremely violent encounter. Some male COs feel women, due to their smaller physical size, will be unable to defend either themselves or their fellow officers should the need arise. This perception among male officers may cause them to become more protective of female officers (Bowersox, 1981; Zimmer, 1986; Kissel and Katsampes, 1980). As one male correctional officer stated:

> "I feel that the majority of females that work with me could not handle a serious confrontation with an inmate so we are constantly watching out for them. There are very few female officers that I would want for a partner" (Walters, 1992b).

Issues of sexuality are also a major concern for some male correctional officers. Sexual issues are generally assumed to be problematic in one of three ways. First, some male COs fear female correctional officers may become victims of sexual assault (Parisi, 1984; Crouch, 1985; Jacobs, 1981). The lack of heterosexual relationships has been termed by Sykes (1958) to be one of the "pains of imprisonment" that must be suffered by incarcerated offenders. Female officers, according to this argument, may become the sexual outlet of choice for men who have been without the sexual company of women for years, and in some cases, decades. This issue can become magnified if the institution houses men convicted of sex offenses. A second concern for some male correctional officers is that female officers could voluntarily engage in sexual assignations with male inmates, thus severely compromising the security of the prison. Finally, there are those who feel that women COs may use their sexuality to curry favor with correctional administrators, thus gaining an unfair advantage in the competition for promotions and desirable assignments (Jurik, 1985; Owen, 1985). A male correctional officer summed up these concerns as follows:

> "I feel that a female should not be in a male prison no more than a male should work in a female prison..... Most of the women in corrections have had sexual relations with inmates or upper echelons in corrections in our institution. I feel it makes a much more dangerous situation for male officers and for other inmates" (Walters, 1992b).

A final concern voiced by some male correctional officers pertains to issues of privacy that may commonly arise in a prison housing male inmates (Alpert, 1984; Horne, 1985; Jacobs, 1981). Correctional officers are responsible for the daily supervision of inmates. This commonly involves observing inmates in showers and bathrooms. Furthermore, one important duty of COs entails conducting searches of inmates. These searches may include "pat-downs", strip searches, and cavity searches. While these procedures are invasive and embarrassing under the best of circumstances, when conducted by a member of the opposite sex they can be easily escalate to humiliation and degradation.

These arguments against employing women correctional officers in male prisons, though held by many, fail on both the basis of logic and the examination of hard data. While *on average* women COs may be physically smaller than males, there are many female officers who are more physically imposing than their male counterparts. Further, one-on-one physical confrontations are generally avoided when possible in a correctional facility. Rather, the preferred mode of dealing with recalcitrant inmates is to attempt to verbally persuade the offender to comply with the COs directives or, failing that, simply employ the use of more COs. Research analyzing inmate assaults on correctional officers in 53 correctional institutions conducted by Ross (1996) found male officers were the victims in 94% of the cases. In addition, Rowan (1996) examined inmate assaults on COs working in maximum security institutions in 48 states and the Federal Bureau of Prisons. In these prisons male officers were 3.6 times as likely to be physically assaulted by inmates than were female COs. While comparable data on sexual assaults by inmates on staff are rare, its is important to note than in many prison riots male correctional officers have been raped. As one women CO commented:

> "All we hear is 'you are going to be raped'. Women are raped on the streets and in homes every day. After all, like I tell these male protectors, I'll get over being raped a lot better than you will" (Walters, 1992b).

The problem of female officers becoming sexually involved with male inmates is of course a possibility, and has in fact happened. However, instances such these are rare, and the same type of security lapse could occur in a homosexual relationship between a male CO and a male inmate. Furthermore, the possibility a female officer might use her feminine wiles to advance her career might take place in a correctional institution, as it could in any industry where male superiors supervise female subordinates. If this logic were used to deny employment opportunities to women, the entire economy could be in peril.

Women officers do, in the course of their duties, sometimes violate the "privacy" of male inmates they are required to supervise. Legally, this is not a real concern, as the courts have consistently ruled inmates have no real constitutionally guaranteed right to privacy. Some correctional agencies have simply dealt with the issue by not assigning female COs to duties inmates may feel intrusive, leaving these responsibilities for male officers to perform.

It is extremely important to note not all male correctional officers are resistant to the employment of women in male prisons, in fact research has shown quite the opposite is true. Kissel and Katsampes (1980) found the majority of male correctional officers receptive to working with women, with 68% reporting very favorable attitudes toward their female co-workers and 32% stating they feel that female COs perform their duties in a very effective manner. Another study reported 80% of male officers agreed that women should be employed as correctional officers, and the acceptance of female officers was increasing at their institution. While these numbers were slightly lower than those of female officers, they were still highly reflective of female CO support (Lawrence and Mahan, 1998). Walters (1993) also observed an openness to hiring female officers among male COs. In a study of four midwestern prisons 58% of male COs held positive attitudes towards their female counterparts, 20% were ambivalent about women COs, and only 22% appeared resistant to working with women. Comments by these male officers included:

> "Having seen both male and female officers handling the same problems every day, it has shown me that sex doesn't matter. The person who handles themself as a professional can be relied upon, and those who don't generally don't last long here. I work everyday with female officers and it is no different than with male officers" (Walters, 1992b).

> "In my six years in corrections a majority of the female COs I have worked with have been, and are, truly professional, capable, and competent in their performance" (Walters, 1992b).

> "I have found the majority of the female corrections officers whom I have worked with to be highly professional, dependable, and most

capable of performing the rigorous and highly stressful job of corrections officer" (Walters, 1992b).

In addition, some research exists which helps differentiate those male correctional officers who are accepting of women in the prison workplace from those who are not (Walters, 1993; Simpson and White, 1985). One important predictor is the quality of working relationships the male officer has experienced with female officers. Those officers who have found working with women was an enjoyable, professional experience were far more likely to welcome women into the CO corps than were those male officers who reported poor working relationships with women co-workers. Male officers who reported higher levels of job satisfaction also seemed to more receptive to women working in prison. Also, male COs who saw the role of corrections as rehabilitative, and those male officers who had attained higher levels of education accepted women officers in the workplace far more than did those officers who were custody-oriented and had lower educational levels. And logically, male officers who worked in prisons that housed female offenders more readily accepted women COs into the workplace.

Yet all the discussion concerning women correctional officers and their utilization in prisons is based on the assumption that male and female correctional officers are in some way different than one another. To ascertain if this is indeed the case, several questions must be answered. Do male and female COs actually possess work related characteristics that vary significantly from one another? Do inmates react to each gender group differently? And finally, do women and men exhibit any meaningful differences in the performance of their role as correctional officers? To answer these questions one must examine the relevant research.

Gender Difference in Work-Related Characteristics

Zupan (1986) observed that few real substantial differences exist in either attitudes or perceptions between men and women employed as correctional officers. However, some differences do consistently appear, and these differences can be important to the functioning of the prison.

Starting in the 1960's and continuing through the 1970's, the correctional philosophy in American prisons underwent an important change. Throughout most of American history prisons were seen as mechanisms for punishing offenders. Any behavioral change that might accrue to an inmate would be the result of individual reformation. Little interest or effort was shown for developing programs that would, as the basic goal of the institution, bring about long-lasting and meaningful change in the attitudes and behaviors of incarcerated offenders. However, by the 1960's *rehabilitation* became the new philosophy of the American correctional system. In order the facilitate the effectiveness of these new programs it was thought imperative correctional officers be employed who would be amenable to these efforts. Some, as mentioned earlier, thought female COs would be more supportive of a rehabilitative ideology and a human service approach to prison operation.. This in fact appears to be the case, with a substantial amount of research bolstering this assertion (Walters, 1992; Jurik, 1985a; Jurik, 1985b; Fry and Glaser, 1987; Jurik and Halemba, 1984). Although by the 1980's the American prison system's ardor for rehabilitation had cooled significantly, it has not completely disappeared, and women correctional officers can be very valuable in assisting inmates in changing their lives.

As the field of corrections attempted to professionalize, more interest was paid to recruiting correctional officers with the skills necessary to manage inmates in more efficient and humane ways. To this end increased emphasis was placed on the employment of officers with higher educational attainment. Several

138

studies (Jurik, 1985a; Jurik, 1985b; Jurik and Halemba, 1984; Walters and Lagace, 1999) have found female correctional officers possessed higher levels of education than did their male CO brethren. This fact is important, as it may explain the aforementioned female officer preference for a rehabilitative approach to corrections. Further, this increased educational attainment may contribute to the ability of female officers to deal with problem inmates in verbal manner, as opposed to the more confrontational and sometimes coercive means common to male correctional officers.

On the other hand, numerous studies have shown women correctional officers are more prone to job-related stress than are their male co-workers (Freeman and Johnson, 1982; Cheek and Miller, 1983; Cullen et al., 1985; Stinchcomb, 1986; Zupan, 1986; Wright and Saylor, 1991; Blau et al., 1986; Gross et al.; 1994). Prisons are not the quiet and orderly institutions many times represented in the media. Rather, they are commonly loud, cacophonous, and chaotic places. Inmates are commonly both argumentative and verbally abusive to staff. The prospect of violence by inmates, either against one another or the COs, is always a distinct possibility. These factors in and of themselves are stressful. Women officers are further subjected to what Jurik (1988) characterized as "gender-related" stress. This form of stress is the consequence of difficulties that result from male correctional officers who are antagonistic to the employment of female COs. This hypothesis is supported by research by Jurik and Halemba (1984), who observed female COs felt that most of their work problems were caused by co-workers. Gross et al. (1994) observed the increased stress felt by women COs manifested itself in several forms. Women officers were more often tardy, absent, and used more sick days than did male officers. While this would generally be indicative of stress, the authors noted it might, at least in part, be the result of the fact that 43% of the female officers were single working mothers. However, female COs were less likely to have filed a stress or inmate assault-related workman's compensation claim. Still, these women COs did report higher stress levels than did their male colleagues. The genders also appeared to handle occupational stress in different ways (Hurst and Hurst, 1997). Male officers processed stress by developing a deliberate plan to change the stress-producing situation. Female officers, however, dealt with stress by seeking either informational, tangible, or emotional support.

While not consistent across a number of prison studies, other work-related gender differences have been observed among correctional officers. For example, women COs appear attracted to their jobs for different reasons than are male officers (Jurik and Halemba , 1984; Rogers, 1991). Males officers seem drawn to prison work for *extrinsic reasons*, such as pay, benefits, and job security. Conversely, women officers seem drawn to corrections for more *intrinsic reasons*, such as helping people and making society a better place to live. Work assignments for female correctional officers also appear to differ from those of males. Both Jurik (1985a) and Horne (1985) noted women COs have more limited duty assignments, such as control rooms, visitation, and clerical work. Other research (Crouch, 1985; Walters, 1992) stated female COs are more often found working in minimum security areas. While these assignments may be safer than working in the living areas of higher-security inmates, being restricted to these duties may limit an officer's opportunities for advancement through the ranks.

Gender Difference in Interaction with Inmates

As discussed previously, many experts in the field of corrections feel women COs can be very effective in dealing with male inmates. Correctional officers themselves, regardless of gender, appear generally supportive of the employment of women COs in prisons housing male offenders (Lawrence and Mahan, 1998; Kissel and Katsampes, 1980; Walters, 1993). However, the opinions of the inmates themselves have rarely been examined. When inmates are asked how they feel about the employment of women correctional officers, their remarks are generally very supportive.

Kissel and Katsampes (1980) questioned inmates at incarcerated in a large Colorado jail about their attitudes pertaining to female COs. Of these inmates 52% reported they had never seen or heard of an inmate trying to shock female officers. Fifty-four percent stated they would be less likely to be physically aggressive toward female officers, while only 11% thought women COs were easier to manipulate. Surprisingly, 43% reported they would take a protective role in regard to female staff. This study also observed 38% of the inmates did not feel the presence of women officers increased sexual frustration and 21% felt the presence of female COs actually decreased sexual frustration. Most inmates (55%) felt the presence of women in the institution had no effect on their sense of privacy. Additionally, the majority inmates had no problem with being supervised by, or taking orders from, a female officer.

Similar reactions from inmates were elicited by Szockyj (1989) at a pre-trial correctional center in Canada. Inmates at this institution stated they responded to orders from female officers more quickly, and with less retaliation, than they did with male COs. Inmates also felt female COs treated them with more respect, and were equal or superior to male COs in cooling down angry inmates, thus avoiding greater problems. However, most inmates said women officers lacked the physical strength required to effectively cope with a fight situation. The majority of inmates did not feel their privacy was threatened by female COs, although the physical layout of the institution was such that officer observation was less intrusive than it might be in other prisons.

Perceived Gender Difference in Job Performance

As discussed previously, it was assumed women correctional officers would being certain positive behavioral characteristics to the prison environment that many male officers perhaps lacked. Yet there is surprising little objective data concerning the relative job performance of women COs as opposed to men (Zimmer, 1986; Philliber; 1987). What information is accessible is generally in the form of subjective evaluations from correctional officers themselves. Although limited, this data is among the most useful available for assessing relative gender performance of COs.

According to Kissel and Katsampes (1980) the majority of male officers they studied felt women made a special contribution to correctional work, they had increased the "livability" of the institution, and had increased their own personal enjoyment of their job. Most males also felt female officers were no more easily manipulated than were male COs. Additionally, male correctional officers reported women could perform the same duties as males and that males and females complimented one another in the performance of their duties. In the same study female officers also felt they were doing a good job. All thought they performed as well as the male officers. The majority stated that being a women had not restricted them in the performance of their duties, and that they were given as much responsibility as were their male counterparts. Most responded that they felt capable of handling most crisis situations. However, 85% of the female COs reported there were some regular duties where they felt inadequate or uncomfortable in performing because they were a woman.

Further information detailing gender variation in job performance is provided by Lawrence and Mahan (1998). In their study of Minnesota COs the majority of both gender groups agreed the presence of women correctional officers improved the prison environment. The majority of both groups also felt women performed well in supervisory position, in judging when to file disciplinary reports on inmates, and in backing up a partner in a dangerous situation. Both groups also agreed women were able to maintain personal control under stress and control verbal confrontations among inmates.

There were, however, certain reservations about women COs expressed in these studies. In both analyses male COs did not evaluate the performance of women officers well in situations involving violence and physical strength. Additionally, while many times the majority of both male and female officers would evaluate the performance of female COs in a positive manner, a higher percentage of female officers evaluated women positively than did male officers.

AFRICAN-AMERICAN CORRECTIONAL OFFICERS

Historically it has been the practice in America to locate prisons in remote, rural locations. Perhaps the reasoning was that cities were the major breeding grounds of crime, therefore a stint in "wholesome" rural American would aid in the reformation of criminals. There were, of course, financial considerations. Land and labor costs in rural areas were frequently lower than in the cities. More likely, the "out of sight, out of mind" philosophy was in operation. Regardless of the reason, the location of prisons in rural locales had consequences for prison staffing. Correctional officers were commonly recruiting locally, many times ensuring that they were white and held rural attitudes and values.

Motivation for the Increased Employment of Black Correctional Officers

While this process was not often seen as problematic, by the 1960's many correctional reformers were calling for change. Two problems had come to beset prisons. First, during this time frame the crime rate in America exploded, causing an attendant massive increase in prison populations. Second, the prison population became disproportionately African-American. Most of these incarcerated blacks were from urban environments, and frequently militant. The stage was therefore set for conflict between rural, white COs and urban, black inmates.

In order to contend with this dilemma, the issue was addressed in two ways. First, an attempt was made to locate correctional facilities nearer to urban areas. This would allow more frequent interaction between inmates, who were predominately urban themselves, and their families and loved ones. Hopefully this interaction would aid in the reintegration process and make the prison experience more bearable for inmates. In addition, an attempt was made to increase the recruitment of urban, black, correctional officers. It was hoped the recruitment of these new officers would lessen the cultural conflict that was seen by some to be the root cause of many prison problems (Carroll, 1988).

Sources of Resistance to Change

Not all in the correctional community were impressed with this reasoning. Johnson (1996) related several reasons why some were opposed to the increased recruitment of African-Americans as correctional officers. Some in corrections felt increased minority recruitment sounded too much like a "quota system", and thus was unfair to majority job candidates. It was also thought these efforts might attract unqualified applicants. These applicants could increase interstaff hostilities, and therefore decrease the morale of the entire correctional officer staff. Additionally, it was thought these efforts could actually be unfair to minority applicants in that they would unfairly be labeled as having only been hired because of their race, rather than because they were truly qualified for the position. One final reason stated by some opposed to increased minority employment concerned security issues. Some felt that by increasing the degree of commonality between inmates and staff, there would be a greater likelihood that prisoners could influence COs in the performance of their daily duties.

However, correctional systems persevered, and their efforts met with some success. By 1994, almost 23% of the correctional officers in America were African-American, up from about 20% ten years earlier. While this number was almost twice the percentage of blacks in the general population, it still lagged far behind the almost 48% of prison inmates that were African-American in 1994.

TABLE 7.2
RACIAL AND ETHNIC DISTRIBUTION OF CORRECTIONAL OFFICERS IN AMERICAN PRISONS 1985 - 2002

	1985*	1990*	1995**	2000**	2002**
Total	92,955	168,972	213,370	254,871	255,860
White	72.6%	69.2%	69.2%	66.4%	65.7%
Black	21.7%	21.8%			23.8%
Hispanic	4.4%	5.3%			8.4%
Other	1.3%	3.7%	30.8%	33.6%	2.1%

1995 and 2000 data do not delineate between non-white groups

*Source: Complied by the author from Bureau of Justice Statistics, *Sourcebook of Criminal Justice Statistics - 1988, 1989, 1990, 1991, 1992, 1993, 1994, 1998*. Washington, DC: U.S. Department of Justice.

**Source: Camp, C. (2003). *The Corrections Yearbook 2002*. Middletown, CT: Criminal Justice Institute.

Racial Variation in Correctional Attitudes

While the logic of the above arguments appear sound, again one must look to the existing research to ascertain their validity. Some research reports that black officers feel better about working with inmates than do their white co-workers. Britton (1997) observed both black and hispanic male officers felt more efficacious in working with inmates. Other research noted black correctional officers appear more accepting of a rehabilitative approach to corrections and more approving of programs for inmates within the institution (Van Voorhis et al., 1991; Cullen et al., 1989; Jackson and Ammen, 1996; Jurik, 1985b). Yet not all researchers have come to the same conclusions. Neither Walters (1995) nor Crouch and Alpert (1982) were able to find any significant differences in punitiveness toward inmates by minority and white COs. Conversely, Jacobs and Kraft (1978) report minority COs were *more* punitive in their attitudes toward inmates than were white officers, as did Walters (1995) in a study of Canadian officers.

In what is perhaps one of the better discussions of racial stereotypes and the correctional officers, Klofas (1986) examined the attitudes of 832 officers working in four maximum security prisons in New York. He found the popular stereotype of white, veteran, rural officers as rigidly custodial and anti-inmate to be false. Further, the stereotype of black, urban, younger officers as more progressive in their view of inmates and correctional philosophy was also false. In fact, neither race nor urbanization was related to a human service approach to corrections. Age, however, was strongly related to this approach, but not in the stereotypically assumed manner. *Older* officers were in fact more interested in a human service approach to prison operation, not younger officers.

It does appear that black correctional officers may be difficult to retain in the CO corps. Jacobs and Grear (1977) Jurik and Winn (1987) and Patenaude

146

and Golden (2000) all noted black officers were more likely to leave the ranks of COs than their white colleagues. This may be the result of their interaction with superiors within the prison hierarchy. Some previously discussed research has noted CO - prison administration conflicts are common (see Chapter 6). However, these frictions appeared greater among black officers (Jacobs and Grear, 1977; Rogers, 1991; Jurik and Winn, 1987) and may therefore contribute disproportionately to their desire to leave the field of corrections.

Summary

Both women and African-Americans have become valued members of the correctional officer corps. While perhaps not fulfilling every preconceived notion of correctional theorists, both groups have made important contributions to the provision of safe and secure prisons for American society. While they may differ in some ways from the "traditional " correctional officer, they are, for the most part, virtually indistinguishable from their fellow COs. Quite possibly, as some criminologists have suggested, organizational factors are just as important in shaping correctional officers' attitudes as are individual officer characteristics (Jurik, 1985b; Walters, 1991). The prison world is a unique and powerful environment, and just as it effects inmates, it can most assuredly effect correctional officers.

Does this mean efforts to recruit and retain women and minorities as COs should be abandoned? Certainly not, and for three important reasons. First, the law demands all individuals be given an equal opportunity for employment. To refuse minorities of any type entrance to a career in corrections denies basic concepts of fairness that characterize modern American society. Second, inmates must be prepared to enter into a multicultural, multisexual world when they are eventually released into free society. By employing minorities of all types as COs, inmates can learn to interact with persons who possess sexual, racial, and ethnic characteristics different from their own. But most significantly, the question should not be "Why employ minorities?". Rather, the question should be "Why not?". When research fails to find many meaningful differences between minority and majority officers, the findings are basically telling us this: there are no reasons not to employ these groups - they are, for the most part, very similar to the officers who have always provided security in our prisons. Each individual officer provides his or her own contribution to the field of corrections, and the contributions of both women officers and African-American officers have been significant.

8

CORRECTIONAL OFFICERS WITHOUT WALLS:
PROBATION & PAROLE OFFICERS

Not all correctional officers are tasked with supervising inmates within correctional facilities. Probation and parole officers are community based officers who provide services to help offenders remain in, or, to be reintegrated into the community. The primary responsibility of probation and parole officers is to ensure that probationers comply with the orders of the court, and parolees comply with the orders of the parole board, while providing access to a variety of programs to help the offender.

Functions

The dual tasks of probation and parole officers, the supervision and rehabilitation of offenders, require a great deal of paperwork and a wide variety of job activities. Probation and parole officers generally come in contact with an offender for the first time after that person has been convicted and sentenced by a court. For a parolee, the first contact may occur when the parolee shows up at the probation and parole office after being released from prison. The first meeting is called the *initial intake*. It is a meeting where the offender/client provides considerable background information to the officer. After the initial interview the officer generally has a limited amount of time (30 days) to prepare a formal report using the Case Management Classification (CMC) system. While completing the CMC an officer will conduct a risk and needs assessment. What risk does the offender pose to the community? What needs are there for the client to successfully complete probation/ parole? Here the officer develops a case plan for the offender. This is where the needs assessment is utilized. An offender may, for example, be required by the court to attend anger management courses. A deadline for enrolling and completing the course would be set by the officer. Failure on the part of the client to complete this course could be grounds to revoke probation and the imposition of the sentence. Probation and parole officers ensure that offenders pay any financial obligation to the court. An officer would establish a repayment plan with the offender. In some jurisdictions the probation and parole officer collects the monies and distributes them accordingly. Probation and parole officers establish a reporting schedule where the offender comes in for an office visit. For some offenders this could include a urinalysis to check for drug usage. Home visits are also part of the reporting schedule. Officers can plan and conduct scheduled and/or unscheduled home visits to ensure the offender is complying with all conditions.

As noted earlier, there is a considerable amount of paperwork involved in probation and parole. In Wisconsin, for example, a probationer or parolee file is divided into 10 sections. Section 1 contains initial intake information with up to 13 different reports. Reports in this section include the chronological log which is used to document every action taken by the officer, the case plan, the CMC booklet and any violation/ revocation summaries. Section 2 is for court papers including judgment of conviction and sentence, restitution orders, and other court documents. Section 3 is devoted to violations. In this section any violation investigation reports are placed as well as corresponding police reports and statements taken about the violation and copies of violation warrants and apprehension requests. Section 4 covers employment and travel requirements or restrictions. Probationers or parolees may move out of state but there is considerable documentation involved in the process. Department of Corrections form 1 (DOC 1) is the Interstate Compact Application and Agreement form. Section 5 is the confidential section which contains medical reports, psychological reports, dental reports, school transcripts as well as chain of evidence/ UA (urine analysis) results. Section 6 is for miscellaneous reports which do not go in any other section. Community service referrals, a community service report, and email messages go in this section. Section 7 is for institution forms such as the inmate release authorization form, the pre-parole investigation report and the waiver of state and individual good time report. Section 8 is devoted to administrative and revocation materials. Section 9 is for sex offender paperwork and the final section of the file is for monthly report forms. In Wisconsin, an offender's file can contain up to 80 different Department of Correction forms as well as many other outside forms such as police reports, medical reports, and many other types of reports.

The following is an example of the conditions of Standard Probation Supervision for probationers in New Mexico, as posted on their website. As a condition of probation convicted offenders agree to abide by the stated conditions. Failure on the part of the probationer to follow those stated conditions can result in a revocation of probation and the offender being sent to prison. Offenders may have more conditions placed on them depending on their background and criminal record. Registered sex offenders in Wisconsin, for example, have 35 or more conditions of supervision.

152

1. **State Laws** - I will not violate any of the laws or ordinances of the State of NM, or any other jurisdiction. I shall not endanger the person or property of another.

2. **Reporting** - I will report to my Probation/Parole Officer as often as required and will submit completed and truthful written reports as required by my Probation/Parole Officer. All communication with my Probation/Parole Officer will be truthful and accurate and I will promptly reply to any correspondence or communication I may receive from the Probation Office.

3. **Status** - I will get permission from my Probation/Parole Officer before: a) Leaving the county where I am being supervised and/or residing; b) Changing jobs; c) Changing residence; or d) Engaging in any major financial contract or debt.

4. **Association** - I will not associate with any person identified by my Probation/Parole Officer as being detrimental to my Probation supervision, which may include persons having a criminal record, other probationers and parolees, and victims or witnesses of my crime or crimes.

5. **Visits** - I will permit any Probation/Parole Officer to visit me at my home or place of employment at any time. I will permit a warrant-less search by the Officer of my person, automobile, residence, property and/or living quarters if he/she has reasonable cause to believe the search will produce evidence of a violation of my conditions of probation.

6. **Employment** - Unless exempted, I will make every effort to obtain and hold a legitimate job and fulfill all financial obligations required of me including support of my family. I shall cooperate with my Probation Officer in any effort to assist me in obtaining employment. If I lose my job for any reason, I shall report this fact to my probation/Parole Officer within 48 hours of the change.

7. **Weapons** - I will not buy, sell, own or have in my possession, at any time, firearms, ammunition, or other deadly weapons.

8. **Drugs** - I will not buy, sell, consume, possess or distribute any controlled

substances except those legally prescribed for my use by a State Certified Medical Doctor. I will also provide urine or breath test specimens for laboratory analysis upon request of the Probation and Parole division.

9. **Arrest** - I will report any arrest, charge or questioning by a Peace Officer to my Probation/Parole Officer within 48 hours of the incident.

10. **Transfer** - If my probation supervision is transferred to another state, I will abide by any additional supervision conditions required by that state.

11. **Informant** - I will not enter into any agreement to act, or act as an "informer" or special agent for any law enforcement agency without the permission of the Director of the Probation and Parole Division and the sentencing judge.

12. **Probation Costs** - I will pay probation costs as determined by my Probation/Parole Officer on or before the designated date each month to the Corrections Department in the form of a money order or cashier's check.

13. **Photo** - I will submit myself for photographing and fingerprinting as directed by the Probation & Parole Division.

14. **Alcohol** - I shall not possess, use or consume any alcoholic beverages and will not at any time enter what is commonly known as a bar or lounge where alcoholic beverages are served or sold for consumption on the premises (New Mexico Department of Corrections, n.d.).

Some states include the condition of accounting for whereabouts and activities, that is, the probationer or parolee must keep this or her supervising agent informed as to where they are and what they are doing. However, the New Mexico rules are very representative of practices in other states.

Probation and Parole Revocation

If a probationer or parolee violates one of the conditions, a probation or parolee officer can initiate the paperwork necessary to revoke probation or parole. In states where the probation and parolee division is part of the department of corrections, which is part of the executive branch of state government, no judicial involvement is needed for revocation of parole. For probation and parolee divisions within a state's department of corrections, probation and parole revocation is solely the discretion of the department of corrections. Probation revocation is dependent upon the type of sentence; withheld, or imposed and stayed. The judiciary involvement in these types of situations occurs only after the revocation has been completed by the department of corrections. The court's involvement is limited by the type of sentence. A *withheld sentence* means the case would be returned to court for the purposes of sentencing. *An imposed and stayed sentence* means that whatever the original sentence, imposed by the court, would then be implemented.

For states in which probation is a function of the judiciary, all revocation action would return to the court of original jurisdiction. A revocation hearing would be held per the guidelines as outlined in *Gagnon v. Scarpelli* (1973) a U.S. Supreme Court case that focused on the rights of a probationer in regards to probation revocation. In some instances where the Parole Board has the authority to revoke parole these Boards must follow the guidelines laid out in *Morrissey v. Brewer* (1972) another U.S. Supreme Court case which focused on the rights of parolees as they relate to revocation. In other words, for states where probation and parole are part of the department of corrections, revocation is an administrative function of the department and the judiciary has a very limited role in the process. For states where the judiciary have control of probation, the revocation process is within the jurisdiction of the court. Either way, the end result is the same - an offender who violated a condition of probation or parole is sent to prison to finish out his or her sentence.

Federal Probation and Pretrial Service Officers

There are 4,516 probation officers and 673 pre-trial service officers at the federal level. Both are employees of the Administrative Office of the U.S. Courts. Federal probation officers conduct pre-sentence investigations and supervise offenders on probation and supervised release (Reaves and Bauer, 2003). At the end of September, 2003, there were 110,621 persons under supervision of probation officers. Of those, 75,680 were serving terms of supervised release following their release from prison and accounting for 68 percent of those under supervision. In 2003, federal probation officers generated over 188,000 reports including 67,744 pre-sentence investigations and 38,569 violation reports (Mecham, 2004). They have statutory authority to arrest supervisees for violations and, if allowed by the federal judicial district, may carry a firearm while on duty. Currently, eight judicial districts do not allow probation officers to carry a firearm. Probation officers receive extensive firearms training from the district firearms instructor who is certified by the Administrative Office of the U.S. Court. Officers who receive firearms training have the option of carrying a weapon or not. Pre-trial service officers conduct investigations of defendants charged with an offense and make recommendations to the court for conditional release or pretrial detention. They do not have statutory authority to arrest nor are they allowed to carry a firearm (Reaves and Bauer, 2003). In 2003, pre-trial service officers activated 97,317 new defendant cases generated 83,798 pre-bail reports, 8,288 other types of reports, and conducted 66,824 interviews (Mecham, 2004).

Probation and pre-trial service offices are located in 93 of the 94 federal district courts. Thirty nine districts have both a probation and pre-trial service office. In 53 districts, probation and pretrial are combined into one office under the control of a chief probation officer. Federal probation and pre-trial services operate through the federal district court. Just like there is a federal marshal appointed for each judicial district there is a chief probation officer and a chief pre-trial officer appointed for each judicial district. While marshals are appointed by the president, deputy marshals are hired through the civil service process. The chief probation officer and the chief pre-trial officer of a district are appointed by the district court, which is administered by the Chief U.S. District Judge, and the chief officers do their own hiring, manage their budgets and have a great deal of autonomy to run their offices. Chief officers advertise, review applications, and interviews prospective employees. The chief probation officer then makes a recommendation to the chief judge, who can concur with, or reject, the recommendation. For pre-trial officers, the hiring process is at the chief level. The chief pre-trial officer of the district does the recruiting and hiring. Federal probation officers and pretrial service officers are not part of the civil service but are eligible for civil service health, life and retirement benefits. Officers are able to retire at age 50 with 20 years of hazardous duty service or at any age with 25 years of hazardous duty under the Federal Employees Retirement System.

The minimum requirements to be a federal probation officer or pretrial officer are: a bachelor's degree, certain physical requirements, have not reached the age of 37 at the time of appointment, and other specialized experience. Training consists of on the job training for the first six months or so and then a week of intense new officer orientation training at the Federal Judicial Center in the nation's capital. Any other training is conducted at the local district level.

As mentioned previously, local administration is through the chief probation and pretrial service officers and the district courts they serve. They ultimately answer to the chief judge of the district. At the national level, the Administrative Office of the United States Courts, under the guidance of the Judicial Conference of the United States, provides oversight and establishes policies and procedure for local probation officers. Within the Administrative Office is the Office of Probation and Pretrial Services, which has 50 staff personnel providing oversight and support to all probation officers. A final group which is very influential is the Chiefs' Advisory Group. This group is made up of eight chief probation officers and chiefs of pre-trial services, who are elected among their peers to represent different regions of the country. This Board provides advice and assistance to the Office of Probation an Pretrial Services on matters including policies, procedures, and programs which would have an impact on the entire federal probation and pretrial system (United States Probation and Pretrial Services System Year in Review Report, 2002).

State and Local Probation and Parole Officers

There are approximately 51,000 state and local probation and parole officers in the United States. Table 9.1 provides a state by state breakdown including probation and parole officers as well as supervisors. If support and other staff are included, the total number of personnel would exceed 72,000.

Probation and parole are highly variable criminal justice practices in this country. In about half the states probation and parole falls under the control of the state's department of corrections while, in other states, parole is a state function and probation is a county responsibility or it is a part of the judiciary. In several states probation and parole are separate state entities. In other states probation and parole officers are considered peace officers and have the power of arrest as well as being able to carry firearms. In other states they are not peace

158

TABLE 8.1
PROBATION AND PAROLE OFFICERS 2000

State	Probation Officer	Parole Officer	P&P Officer	State	Probation Officer	Parole Officer	P&P Officer
Alabama			276	Nebraska	188	22	
Alaska			95	Nevada			248
Arizona	1,113	103		New Hampshire			76
Arkansas			281	New Jersey	1,486	432	
California	5,000	3,150		New Mexico			209
Colorado	669	99		New York	2,640	1,337	
Connecticut	280	68		North Carolina			2,078
Delaware			342	North Dakota			52
Florida			3,063	Ohio			929
Georgia	1,041	477		Oklahoma			321
Hawaii		30		Oregon	n/a		
Idaho			154	Pennsylvania			530
Illinois	2,900	303		Rhode Island			67
Indiana		76		South Carolina			778
Iowa			442	South Dakota	89	27	
Kansas	343	147		Tennessee			709
Kentucky			358	Texas	5,900	1,779	
Louisiana			650	Utah			330
Maine			81	Vermont			275
Maryland			809	Virginia			867
Massachusetts	1,452	184		Washington			790
Michigan			931	West Virginia	167		
Minnesota			300	Wisconsin			1,815
Mississippi			245	Wyoming			88
Missouri			1,450	Federal	4,516		

Source: Camp, C. (2002). *The Corrections Yearbook 2001*. Middleton, CT: Criminal Justice Institute, Inc. States which did not provide information for this table were either called by the authors for current numbers or corresponded with via e-mails.

officers nor do they have the power of arrest. In some states they are not considered peace officers but have limited power of arrest. In states which allow officers to carry a firearm, some require officers to be armed while on duty and in others it is optional.

Either way, the officer must receive firearms training in the basic academy and qualify annually to continue to carry a weapon. Regardless of how probation and parole officers are organized, or whether or not they can carry a firearm or make an arrest, there are some commonalities of all probation and parole officers. They are tasked to protect the public and supervise offenders who are serving their sentence in the community.

There are three different ways for probation and parole officers to be employed. One is within the executive branch of government at the state level. Another is under county government, and the third is directly under the control of the court, or a combination thereof. In 25 states probation and parole offices are employees of the state department of corrections. A second method is for parole officers to be state agents, and probation officers to be county employees or employed by the state court system. Under this system, in thirteen states parole officers are state employees while probation officers are employed by the state court system or the county government. The third method is where agents are employed by the state, but are not part of the department of corrections. Eight states use this method of employment, where probation and parole officers are state employees, but are under different state organizations rather than the state department of corrections.

Wisconsin, with over 1800 agents, is an example of the first method. Adult probationers and parolees are the responsibility of the Division of Community Corrections within the Department of Corrections employed by the state of Wisconsin within the executive branch. In Michigan, it is the Field Operations Administration within the Department of Corrections. In Texas, parolees are supervised by the Parole Division of the Texas Department of Criminal Justice while probationers are administered by the Community Justice Assistance Division of the Texas Department of Criminal Justice. Figure 8.1 provides a list of states in which probation and parole supervision is an element of the state executive branch and represents an element of the state's department of corrections. It is the department which sets the conditions of probation and parole and it is the department which revokes probation or parole.

FIGURE 8.1
STATES WITH PROBATION AND PAROLE WITHIN STATE
DEPARTMENT OF CORRECTIONS

Alaska	Michigan	North Dakota	Vermont
Delaware	Mississippi	Ohio	Virginia
Florida	Missouri	Oklahoma	Washington
Idaho	Montana	Rhode Island	Wisconsin
Iowa	New Hampshire	Texas	Wyoming
Kentucky	New Mexico	Louisiana	Utah
North Carolina			

Source: American Probation and Parole Association (n.d.) *Adult Probation and Parole Directory*. Retrieved September 1, 2004, from http://www.appa-net.org/directory.

Figure 8.2 provides a list of states which have a state level parole department and local or judicial probation offices. In Arizona, for example, adult parole services are provided by the Division of Community Corrections within the state department of corrections, whereas adult probation services are the function of the state court system. Colorado is similar to Arizona in that parolees are under the supervision of the state department of corrections while probationers are under the supervision of the Colorado Judicial Department. In California, on the other hand, the state provides services for parolees while the counties provide services for probationers. Illinois probation services are administered by the circuit court in its 102 counties. Parolees are administered by the Community Service Division of the state department of corrections. In West Virginia, like the states where parolees are supervised by some element of the department of corrections, probationers fall under the control of the Supreme Court of Appeals' probation officers.

FIGURE 8.2
STATES WITH STATE PAROLE DEPARTMENTS
& LOCAL OR JUDICIAL CONTROL OF PROBATION

Arizona	Illinois	Nebraska
California	Indiana	New Jersey
Colorado	Kansas	South Dakota
Connecticut	Massachusetts	West Virginia
Hawaii		

Source: American Probation and Parole Association (n.d.) *Adult Probation and Parole Directory*. Retrieved September 1, 2004, from http://www.appa-net.org/directory.

Nine states have a system where there is a state level probation department and a separate parole board or division supervises its parolees. In Alabama the Board of Pardons and Paroles grants paroles for inmates and it also administers probation through district offices. In Arkansas, it is the Board of Correction and Community Punishment which is the paroling authority and the Department of Community Punishment administers probation. For Georgia, the Board of pardons and Paroles supervises parolees while the Community Corrections Division of the state's Department of Corrections is responsible for probationers. In Pennsylvania, it is the Board of Probation and Parole while in New York the Board of Parole is the paroling authority and the Division of Probation and Correctional Alternatives within the executive branch oversees probation and alternatives to incarceration for that state. In South Carolina there is only one entity and that is the Board of Probation, Parole and Pardon Services. In Tennessee there are two branches of the Board of Probation and Parole. Parolees are supervised through the Parole Field Services. The Division of Field Services supervises adult probationers. Figure 8.3 displays state level probation and parole boards/divisions.

FIGURE 8.3
**STATES WITH STATE LEVEL PROBATION AND PAROLE BOARDS/
DIVISIONS**

Alabama	Maryland	Pennsylvania
Arkansas	Nevada	South Carolina
Georgia	New York	Tennessee

Source: American Probation and Parole Association (n.d.) *Adult Probation and Parole Directory*. Retrieved September 1, 2004, from http://www.appa-net.org/directory.

The three remaining states have somewhat different types of systems. Maine has a state level probation service but no parole agency. Parole was abolished there in 1976 but in 1998 a new program called "supervised community confinement" was implemented. Prisoners with less than a year left on their sentences can apply, and if accepted, are supervised by probation officers. Minnesota has both state and county probation officers, one-third are state probation officers and the rest are county employees. In Oregon the state funds county probation officers.

Many states require probation and parole officers to have as a minimum level of education of at least a bachelor's degree in criminal justice, or a related field. Initial entry-level training varies by state. Probation and parole officers, just like correctional officers in prisons and jails, have the right to use force- up to and including deadly force in the course of their duties. Probation and parole officers have the right to use deadly force to protect their lives or the lives of others. The use of deadly force in other situations is dictated by state law.

Nine states do not allow probation officers the power of arrest. Fifteen states allow officers the power to arrest probationers under their supervision. Many other states consider probation officers to be peace officers and, therefore, have general powers of arrest. In most states where a probation officer is granted peace officer status this status is also granted to parole officers. Only two states, Arizona and Connecticut, award peace officer status to probation officers but not parole officers. Only New Jersey confers peace officer status on parole officers and not to probation officers. Parole officers may have general powers of arrest or limited powers of arrest. Twenty-three states allow parole officers general powers of arrest while fourteen states allow parole officers the power of arrest only for parolees in general, or parolees under their supervision. In six states neither probation officers nor parole officers have the power of arrest.

Sixteen states do not allow adult probation officers from carrying a firearm on duty. Twelve states prohibit adult parole officers from being armed. In Alaska probation and parole officers are required to carry a .40 caliber issued by the department. They may purchase their own, but it must be 9mm or larger. Carrying a firearm is Arizona is optional. In that state probation and parole officers are still considered peace officers whether they are armed or not. In Connecticut, probation officers are considered peace officers with the power of arrest but are not allowed to carry a firearm. In states where carrying a firearm is allowed officers receive firearms training. Probation officers in Maine receive their firearms training from the firearms Training Unit at the Maine State Prison and must qualify annually. In Georgia, probation officers receive 16 hours of firearms training as part of their 160 hour basic probation officer training. All training hours are Peace Officer Standard Training (POST) certified. Probation and parole officers in Mississippi have the option of carrying a firearm. They are certified law enforcement officers and have the power to arrest. All officers receive firearms training from the State Police Academy and also receive firearms training for the Department of Corrections. The department provides a weapon. In Missouri, on the other hand, adult probation and parole officers are not considered as peace officers but they have the power to arrest probationers and parolees and have the option to carry a firearm or not. If they choose to do so, they provide their own weapon and the state provides the ammunition. Two states which do not classify probation and parole officers as peace officer are Kansas and Indiana. Neither state grants probation or parole officers the power of arrest nor do they allow officers to be armed. Wisconsin and Wyoming are similar in the sense that probation and parole officer are not considered peace officers. They can not carry a firearm, but probation and parole officers have the power to arrest offenders on their caseload who are probationers and parolees.

Overall, according to the American Probation and Parole Association (APPA) survey there are 38 jurisdictions in which some or all officers carry a weapon. Three states limit the carrying of firearms to special duty officers. In Kansas, for example, only parole officers who are designated as Special Enforcement Officers are allowed to carry a firearm. Thirteen states require all probation officers to be armed and 20 states require all parole officers to be armed. In 22 states it is optional for probation officers to be armed and it is optional in 20 states for parole officers. In Ohio and West Virginia it is a local decision to arm probation officers because they are part of the local or county judiciary. In West Virginia, two circuit court judges have authorized probation officers to carry weapons in their districts. The most popular caliber handguns probation and parole officers carry are 9mm and .40 calibers. These two calibers are the most common pistols that departments furnish to officers. In states where it is up to officers to provide their own handgun, .38 caliber and .357 caliber revolvers are commonly approved weapons for officers to carry. Again, in states which allow officers to carry a personal handgun the state provides the ammunition.

Duties and Responsibilities

As mentioned previously, probation and parole officers are tasked to protect the public and supervise offenders. As examples, the mission of the North Carolina Division of Community Corrections is to "protect the safety of citizens in our communities throughout the state by providing viable alternatives and meaningful supervision to offenders placed in our custody". The Division's goal is to "accomplish our mission by reaching an equal balance of control and treatment for offenders that will positively affect their behavior and lifestyle patterns" (North Carolina Department of Corrections, n.d.). In Idaho, community corrections "provides offenders the opportunity to make a positive transition into the community by providing individual support and programs and assistance. Accountability and protection are provided by prescribing individual case management plans that are facilitated, monitored and supervised through as assigned probation/parole officer" (Idaho Department of Corrections, n.d.). In Kentucky, "the primary function of the Division of Probation & Parole is to protect the citizens of the Commonwealth through the supervision of offenders who have been placed on probation or parole" (KY Corrections, n.d.). Similarly, the mission of the New Mexico Probation/Parole Division is "to provide for public safety through a balance of supervision, enforcement and the provision of program services to increase the probability of offenders becoming law-abiding citizens" (New Mexico Corrections Department, n.d.). To accomplish this mission the Division has a dual perspective: to enforce the conditions of probation and parole, and to provide services to assist the offender's rehabilitation and re-entry into the community (New Mexico Corrections Department, n.d.).

In order to achieve these daunting goals, probation and parole officers are required to fill several diverse roles. Strong (1981) describes the multiplicity of work tasks that an officer must master. *Detection* involves the supervision of inmates. Officers must be able to tell when the offender is in danger of recidivating and, therefore, putting the community at risk. This involves noting both identifying problem areas endangering the rehabilitative process and seeking to ameliorate them. Being a *broker* involves directing the offender to programs in the community that prove beneficial to the offender's success. Utilizing community programs helps reintegrate the offenders into society, while not forcing probation/parole programs to "reinvent the wheel" and to duplicate services readily available locally. Knowledge of what rehabilitative programs are available in the community is important for fulfilling this role. Officers must also act as *advocates* for offenders in their charge at some times. In some cases, they must assist offenders in fighting for their rights as citizens. "Going to bat" for an offender helps remove obstacles, legal or otherwise, that may hamper the rehabilitative process. To act as an *evaluator*, probation and parole officers need to develop the skills necessary to gather and assess information of many types, develop priorities, balance alternatives, and be able to make a correct decision based on this information. An effective probation and parole officer will also be a *mobilizer*, a person able to motivate persons (both offenders and others), existing community groups and organizations, and gather necessary resources and support within the community in order to facilitate the rehabilitation process. Functioning as an *enabler*, an officer must provide support for an offender's efforts at behavioral change. He or she must be aware of changes in the offender's behavior, reinforce pro-social activity, while being on the lookout for signs that the offender may be at risk for further criminal activity. Hopefully, by helping the offender gain self-insight, by modifying behaviors, and by helping change perceptions and values, the rehabilitation process stands a better chance of success. Further, a successful probation and parole officer must be an *information manager.* He or she must collect and analyze data pertaining to both the community and the offender's case in order to help bring about the successful reintegration of the offender back into the community. As a *mediator,* an officer many times is required to reduce conflicts between people and the community as a whole, or between interest groups within the community. As a neutral actor, it is hoped that an officer can bring his/her special skills to bear on reducing these types of problem situations. Probation and parole officers must also act as *educators,* helping to convey information to offenders, and as *community planners,* assisting community groups and government agencies to develop programs that help offenders achieve their rehabilitative goals. Finally, probation and parole officers must fill the role of *enforcer,* monitoring the behavior of the offender in the community and initiating revocation action against those offenders who fail to abide by rules or continue to threaten the community with their anti-social behaviors.

Problem Areas for Probation and Parole Officers

Probation and parole officers perform the dual functions of law enforcement and rehabilitation. Purkiss, Kifer, Hemmens and Burton (2003) indicate that this leads to role conflict. These officers are supposed to help their clients, while at the same time ensuring public safety. The original goal of probation was to rehabilitate the offender and this remained so until the 1970s when it begin to shift toward increased community protection and offender control. Research by Purkiss et al. (2003) reviewed how statute-defined roles of probation officers changed over the last 10 years. By the early 1990's, the community protection/offender control view of supervision was solidly entrenched in probation. This research was undertaken to see if states had changed the goals of probation. The study revealed "that there were 23 prescribed duties/functions for probation officers" (2003: 13). These functions ranged from writing pre-sentence investigations (23 states), serving warrants (15 states) to supervision (46 states). Analysis revealed nine states had the same number of tasks in 2002 as they did in 1992. Twelve states reduced the number of tasks. Idaho, for example, reduced the number of functions from seven to one. On the other hand, 29 states increased the duties of probation officers. Delaware, for example went from three (supervision, investigation of cases and writing PSI's) to 14. Oregon, which had no tasks in 1992, had eight statutorily mandated tasks by 2002 (Purkiss et al., 2003: 12). Interpreting this data the authors concluded that presently "probation officers are more likely to be statutorily mandated to perform law enforcement tasks than to perform rehabilitative tasks" (Purkiss et al., 2003: 12). So, within the last 30 years the focus has shifted from a priority of rehabilitative efforts to that of law enforcement and control. Duffee and O'Leary developed a correctional policies model to explain the amount of emphasis probation leaders place on the offender and the community. The *Rehabilitation Model* is "characterized by a high emphasis on the individual offender and low emphasis on the community" (1986: 91), historically the role of probation. The *Restraint Model* is "characterized by minimal concern for both community and the offender" (1986: 92), while the *Reintegration Model* stresses both the community and the offender. The *Reform Model* "is characterized by maximum emphasis on community and standards and minimum emphasis on the individual offender" (1986: 89). According to Duffee and O'Leary "the organization's mission to make sure that the offender does not cause the community any more inconvenience, expense, or injury" (1986: 89). The Purkiss et al. (2003) research on state-mandated tasks for probation officers substantiates Duffee and O'Leary's Reform Model, where the emphasis is placed more on the law enforcement/control role rather than the rehabilitative role. The goals of probation have shifted. This is evident by the fact that currently 41 states allow probation or parole officers the power of arrest and 38 states allow either probation or parole officers to carry firearms.

In a study of probation and parole officers in Missouri, Seiter and West (2003) surveyed officers working in the Eastern Region of Missouri. One hundred fourteen completed surveys were returned and eleven in-depth interviews were conducted to determine how probation and parole officers spent their time supervising offenders involving casework and surveillance activities. Casework supervision was defined as "an emphasis on assisting the offender with problems, counseling, and working to make sure the offender successfully completes supervision" (2003: 61). This is the traditional role of probation, or Duffee and O'Leary's (1986) Rehabilitation Model. Surveillance supervision "means an emphasis on monitoring and enforcing compliance with the rules of supervision and the detection of violations leading to revocation and return to custody" (2003: 61). The continuing move toward the law enforcement function, as characterized by Duffee and O'Leary's Reform Model, was demonstrated in this research. Seiter and West (2003) asked respondents to report the amount of time each officer spent on 15 supervisory activities ranging from making home visits to seeing offenders in the office to writing violation reports. Probation and parole officers in Missouri spend about half of their time on four supervisory activities. Officers spent on average 16.4 percent of their time on counseling offenders, followed by 13.6 percent of their time writing violation reports. The third most frequent supervisory activity was conducting offender assessments (11.4%), and they spent almost a tenth of their time (9.2%) trying to place offenders in programs. The other nine activities accounted for the other 50 percent of their time. These activities included making home visits (8%), work visits (1%), conducting drug tests (6.4%), explaining/enforcing rules (8.3%), conducting detention interviews (3.8%), and running offender groups (0.8%). So, probation and parole officers in Missouri spend about 25 percent of their time on just two case supervision activities (counseling offenders, & placing/offenders in programs), and about 25 percent of their time on surveillance supervision activities (writing violation reports & conducting offender assessments). At least in Missouri, according to Seiter and West (2003), probation and parole officers spend slightly more time on casework supervisory activities (55.9%) and slightly less than half of their time on surveillance supervisory activities (41.4%). When asked to rate their own supervisory style, an analysis of data revealed officers had a balanced supervisory style.

Currently, 23 states require probation officers to write Pre-Sentence Investigation reports (PSI's). In Idaho, for example, PSI's are conducted by investigators to gather relevant information about offenders in order to assist the judicial system in selecting among sentencing alternatives (Idaho Department of Corrections, n.d.). Federal probation officers are also tasked with conducting PSI's. Federal presentence reports contain information about the offense, the offender (including ability to pay fines and restitution), impact of the offense on the victim, and sentencing options under the federal sentencing guidelines. The primary purpose of a presentence report is to "provide information that enables the court to impose a fair sentence that satisfies the punishment, deterrence and corrective goals of sentencing." Probation officers "consider applicable statutes and sentencing guidelines apply them to the facts of the case and comes up with a recommended sentence and a justification of it" (Office of Probation and Pretrial Services, 2003: 1). In 2003, federal probation officers completed 67,744 pre-sentence investigations for the courts (Mecham, 2004).

Probation and parole officers, just like law enforcement officers and corrections officers, are involved in a "people business." Co-workers, supervisors, the general public, and offenders all place demands upon an officer. Stress has been defined as "a nonspecific response of the body to any demand" (Slate, Wells, & Johnson, 2003, p. 520). Stress on the job results from the interaction of the worker and the conditions of work (Stress at work, n.d.).

Attitudes in the American Workplace VII the Seventh Annual Labor Day Survey conducted for the Marlin Company by Harris Interactive (2001) reported that:

*82% of workers were at least a little stressed at work with 6% extremely stressed.

*50% said they and fellow workers have a more demanding workload than last year.

*38% feel more pressure at work than last year

*35% say their job is negatively affecting their physical or emotional well being

*48% have too much work to do and/or too many unreasonable deadlines

*42% say that job pressures interfere with family or personal life

*42% say they at least sometimes do not have adequate control or input over work duties

*30% say conditions at work are at times unpleasant pr even unsafe

*36% sometimes find it difficult to express opinions or feelings about job conditions to their superiors.

*26% rarely or never receive appropriate recognition or rewards for good performance

*and 19% say that in the past year, they have witnessed or been aware of bullying - that is physical or verbal bullying - in their workplace.

On the job accidents, absenteeism, employee turnover, diminished productivity and a host of other issues resulting from job stress cost U.S. industry over $300 billion annually (Job Stress, n.d.). This report goes on to state "40% of job turnover is due to stress," that "replacing the average employee costs between $3,000 and $13,000," and that "60-80 % of accidents on the job are stress related" (Job Stress, n.d: 5).

Champion (1999) identifies seven sources of stress among probation and parole officers. They are: job dissatisfaction, role conflict, role ambiguity, officer - client interactions, excessive paperwork and performance pressures, low self-esteem and poor public image, and job risks and liabilities. Job dissatisfaction can occur as a result of many factors such as "low pay, burgeoning caseloads, and unchallenging work" (Champion, 1999: 393-394). Role conflict can occur with the conflicting goals of probation and parole which are "rehabilitation and enforcement" while trying to help the offender become a productive member of society and, at the same time, ensuring that the offender is obeying all of the conditions. Being a blend of part social worker and part police officer can be a stressful situation for many probation and parole officers. Is success measured by when an offender completes his or her sentence without problems or is it measured by when the offender's probation is revoked and must serve out the rest of their sentence in prison? Role ambiguity is another source of stress for probation and parole officers. It is closely related to role conflict. Champion (1999: 395) states "role ambiguity occurs whenever POs have inadequate or even conflicting information about their work roles, the scope and responsibilities of the job." Should more emphasis be placed on the rehabilitative role or the enforcement role? Do departmental mission statements provide enough guidance for the day-to-day activities of officers? Mills (1990: 37) states "the probation officer's work is largely intangible, and he lacks a clear standard by which to measure progress." Mills (1990: 37) further states,

In corrections, practitioners frequently encounter the term "success rate" for probation officers, this normally refers to the number of clients who complete supervision successfully. When it comes to supervision this may or may not be a good way to recognize quality work. Low revocation rates may reflect good supervision or could suggest that the officer is not demanding client accountability. Low revocation rates are common to those probation departments that are so overwhelmed by cases that they cannot possibly do justice to supervision. On the other hand, revocation rates tend to rise when manning increases to allow officers to begin to monitor their clients appropriately.

The problem, according to Mills (1990), goes back to the dual role of the officer - rehabilitating the offender and protecting society. He goes on to say that "the problem, of course, centers on the lack of clarity that surrounds the objectives of supervision..... a positive result may be different from one case to another - termination or revocation - and much is left to the officer's discretion" (1990: 37). Mills is talking about both role conflict and role ambiguity.

Contact with a client can also contribute to job stress. Champion (1999) identifies this problem as "officer - client interaction." Burrell (2000: 1) writes that probation and parole officers "deal with clients who are forced to be there, are unmotivated at best and hostile, uncooperative, and down-right nasty at worst." Throw in the fact that many clients have long-term problems "such as chronic addictions, mental disorders, behavioral problems, assaultive and violent behavior, and lack of employment and basic life skills" (Burrell, 2000: 1), the amount of stress between the officer and the client can be considerable. No wonder Burrell bemoans the fact that probation and parole staff are stressed. Slate et al. (2003: 519) state "probation is a people business, oftentimes requiring intense, stressful confrontations with recalcitrant offenders." A probation/ parole officer may supervise the same recalcitrant offender for years through office visits, work site visits and home visits. Depending upon the conditions, an officer may need to collect urine samples or be required to collect payments for fines or restitution. These contacts can last for months or years.

Excessive paperwork and performance pressures are the fifth source of stress among probation and parole officers. Slate et al. (2003) provides an excellent literature review of probation officer stress. According to these authors numerous studies have reported that excessive paperwork is a stressor. Ballock (2001: 43), a federal probation officer, reports that federal probation officers "have become - in many instances - little more than overpaid biographers." Probation and parole officers in Missouri spend 25 percent of their time on just two activities, writing violation reports (13.6%) and conducting assessment of offenders (11.4%) (Seiter and West, 2003). As was mentioned earlier in the chapter there is a considerable amount of paperwork in this field. Client files in Wisconsin, which are divided into 10 sections, can contain up to 80 different DOC forms, not including any other forms or reports for outside agencies. A long-term client's file could contain hundreds pages of documentation. Each contact with a client, and each activity performed must be documented by the officer.

Champion (1999) identifies low self-esteem and poor public image as other sources of stress. One method of over-coming low self-esteem and poor public image is to attract better qualified applicants. Many states and federal probation agencies have raised the minimal education level to that of a bachelor's degree. In addition starting salaries are competitive with other occupations requiring a similar level of education.

The final sources of stress identified by Champion (1999) are job risks and liabilities. Working with clients who have been convicted of serious crimes can pose a risk to probation and parole officers. Stale et al. (2003) reported that dangers inherent to the job have been identified as stressor for probation officers.

Probation and parole officers many times fall victim to burnout. Champion identifies fifteen different definitions of burnout. The most common elements are "emotional, mental, and physical exhaustion which debilitates and weakens the ability to cope with situations" (1999: 394). According to Slate et al. (2003), numerous studies report a curvilinear relationship between stress or burnout and work experience. Those at the beginning of their careers and those at the end of their careers experience less stress or burnout than those in the middle of their careers. Slate, Johnson and Wells (2000: 57) reported that in one study burnout was "greatest for those who had been on the job between 6 months and three years."

Burrell (2000: 2) argues that it is "the internal workings of the organization and its relationship to the external environment" that creates most of the stress for probation and parole officers. Burrell (2000: 14) suggests that it is "the agency that burns out probation and parole officers not the work." He goes on to espouse three new "conventional wisdoms" about stress:

1. The nature of probation and parole: the work is not what causes burnout, rather, the work is what provides job satisfaction and motivates officers.

2. The nature of PPOs: people go into this work because they like to work with people. Should they stay beyond the first year or so, they know what the job entails and want to do it anyway.

3. The nature of probation and parole agencies: the organization and how it is managed is the critical variable in PPO stress and burnout. Managed well, organizations can mitigate effectively a great deal of stress and still provide a satisfying and motivating environment (Burrell, 2000: 14).

What can be done to reduce stress? Champion (1999) suggests that participatory management is one method to reduce job stress. This involves subordinates providing substantial input for decision making purposes. He also suggests increasing officer input for offender supervision and treatment.

Management By Objective (MBO) involves employees and supervisors setting objectives for the employee to achieve. Regardless of the name, it appears that employee involvement in goal setting and in the decision-making process helps reduce burnout and job stress.

In his research on officer stress, Burrell (2000) places the bulk of the responsibility for reducing stress on management, since most stress results from action of the organization. He developed a list of eleven actions management can take to create a healthier organization and reduce stress (Burrell, 2000: 13-14):

1) Establish clear direction as to role and purpose: everyone should understand the organization's mission and their role in accomplishing that mission. Organizational mission statements help clarify this.

2) Manage proactively, not reactively.

3) Establish priorities; management must make it clear what has to get done and in what order of importance.

4) Ensure stability and constancy; management should try and buffer the organization from unreasonable demands and unwarranted changes, particularly from outside sources.

5) Be consistent; there should be standardization and uniformity across the organization.

6) Manage with fairness, trust and integrity; management should model this behavior relentlessly, set the example in everything you do.

7) Enforce accountability; at all levels of the organization. It flows upward and downward. Management is accountable to staff for guidance, tools, training, resources, and support they need to do the job.

8) Delegate authority and responsibility; staff should have autonomy to act without excessive oversight from leaders.

9) Provide proper resources; staff need the tools and resources to accomplish their missions and objectives and management must ensure those tools

and resources are available.

10) Communicate; communication must be constant, pervasive and two way. It must run up, down and across the organization, and

11) Foster participatory decision making; involvement of staff is essential. They must understand what is happening and why a decision was made. Individuals who know what is going on, have input into the decision making process, and have the authority to complete a task, have increased levels of job satisfaction.

Probation and Parole Officer Typologies

More than 2.2 million adults entered probation supervision in 2003, requiring probation and parole officers to generate hundreds of thousands of presentence investigations. As mentioned earlier, 23 states mandate presentence investigations. In smaller probation offices all officers may be tasked to conduct presentence investigations. In larger probation offices specialized units have been formed to conduct presentence investigations. Rosecrance (1987), in his study of presentence probation investigators, developed a typology of five different styles of investigators based on interviews with presentence investigators from three states. According to Rosecrance about 30 % of the investigators were what he termed *team players*. The assumed role of these officers was to facilitate department policies, the purpose of sentencing was to reflect society's values, and presentence recommendations were non-controversial. They used "bland, innocuous and prosaic syntax in their reports," wanted to ensure their reports would not "cause waves," and included "an excess of social data" (1987: 167). The second type, *the mossback,* accounted for about 30 percent of the officers. These officers "demonstrate a superficial commitment to their jobs by fulfilling minimum requirements and following departmental regulations" (1987: 168). The assumed role of a mossback was following the rules, the purpose of sentencing was to resolve the matter, and the presentence recommendation was the middle of the road. Many, but not all, in this group were older workers putting in time until retirement. The third group of officers identified by Rosecrance were the *hardliners*. They accounted for about 20 percent of all officers. The goal of this group of officers was to protect society and they saw themselves as "bastions of order in an overly permissive world. They believe laws must be enforced with continual vigilance" (Rosecrance, 1987: 69). For this group the assumed role is upholding traditional values, the purpose of sentencing is to deter others, and presentence recommendation is strict. They "see themselves as eminently fair" (Rosecrance, 1987: 169). The fourth group of officers were labeled the *bleeding heart liberals*, who accounted for about 10 percent of the officers. These individuals "contend that the system is so weighted against the defendant that it is incumbent upon them to even up the odds" (Rosecrance, 1987: 170). Their assumed role is to "stick up" for the underdog. The purpose of sentencing is to rehabilitate the offender, and the presentence recommendation should be lenient. This group "holds that society is best served if defendants are improved and changed through their court experience" (Rosecrance, 1987: 168). The final group is comprised of *mavericks* and they account for about 10 percent of all officers. Mavericks are in a search for individual justice. "They attempt to evaluate every case on its own merits" and "conceive themselves as objective judicial advisors and not advocates of a particular point of view" (Rosecrance, 1987: 171). The assumed role of these officers is to weigh the cases' individual merits, the purpose of sentencing is to see that justice is done, and the presentence recommendation is therefore varied.

Another typology of probation and parole officers was developed by Allen et al. (1979). This fourfold model categorizes probation and parole officers based on their attitudes toward the offender and community safety. The *punitive/law enforcement officer* is primarily concerned with the protection and welfare of society. They therefore are interested in controlling the offender, and efforts to rehabilitate the offender are of secondary importance. The *welfare/therapeutic officer,* on the other hand, has a primary interest in the rehabilitative aspects of community-based corrections. These officers tend to see the improvement of the condition of offenders as their most important task. The third type, the *protective/synthetic officer,* attempts to balance these two, sometimes competing, goals. Finally, the *passive/time server officer,* has little interest in either of these two activities. Rather than being concerned with neither offenders nor society, this type of "civil servant" is primarily interested in retaining employment with minimal effort.

Researchers have examined various aspects of probation and parole. Rosecrance's (1987) study, for example, focused only on presentence investigators. He was able to identify five different personality types characterizing how officers viewed their role as probation officers. This typology was based on how officers viewed the role of the presentence report, what the purpose of sentencing was, and what the recommendations were. The Purkiss et al (2003) study focused on 23 legally proscribed functions, which ones were mandates by each individual state, and how mandates changed over time. Seiter and West (2003) explored how some probation and parole officers in Missouri spent their time on 15 different supervisory activities. Duffee and O'Leary (1986) provided four correctional policy models ranging from low emphasis on the community and the offender to high emphasis on both. In the last thirty years the emphasis has shifted from rehabilitating the offender (Rehabilitation Model) to law enforcement and offender control (Reform Model). If Rosecrance's study was replicated today results would probably show a higher percentage of officers who were hardliners and smaller groups of bleeding hearts and mavericks. For the

180

time being, in Missouri, probation and parole officers are spending more time on casework (rehabilitation efforts) supervisory activities than on surveillance (law enforcement/offender control) supervisory activities.

In addition to writing presentence reports, probation and parole officers are, in 46 states, tasked with the supervision of probationers and parolees. Probation and parole officers also provide investigative services to the courts and other agencies, rehabilitation services to offenders, and assistance in employment and home placement. Other common duties include court appearances and testimony, reports to the releasing authorities, home visits, conducting urinalysis, transporting prisoners, referring offenders to appropriate resources, and monitoring payment fees and community service work.

Summary

There are about 56,000 federal, state and local probation and parole officers supervising almost 5 million probationer and parolees. Probation and parole officers provide a wide variety of functions and tasks. In some states they are considered peace officers with powers of arrest and the authority to carry a firearm, while in other states they are not considered as peace officers, nor can they carry a firearm. In other states they have a combination of powers and authority. In about half the states probation and parole officers are considered employees of the state department of corrections within the executive branch of government. In other states probation officers are employed by the courts or are part of the state judiciary. These states have a separate parole division within the state government. The third method of employment is where states have separate state level probation and parole divisions. Within the last 30 years probation and parole philosophy has shifted from the rehabilitation of offenders to an emphasis on law enforcement or control of offenders. Still, probation and parole officers spend about an equal amount of time on rehabilitative or casework activities and law enforcement/ control or surveillance activities. Probation and parole in this country is truly a mixed lot, and the officers who work in these organizations face many of the same problems as do their incarcerated brethren.

9

CURRENT ISSUES CONCERNING CORRECTIONAL OFFICERS

Several changes are taking place in the criminal justice system which will have a great impact upon the working world of correctional officers. These include the unionization of correctional officers, the privatization of corrections, the risks of infectious diseases in the prison environment, violence and the use of force, the development of emergency response teams in prisons, and the "professionalization" of correctional officers

Unions

The unionization of public servants has its beginnings with police fraternal associations in the early 1900s. By 1919, over 30 police departments had been granted charters by the American Federation of Labor (AFL). Officers banded together for welfare benefits such as insurance policies and death benefits, as well as the right to engage in collective bargaining. In Boston, the average wage for a patrolman was $1,300 a year. Officers worked between seventy-three and ninety-eight hours a week with one day off every fifteen days. Days-off were often spent on stand-by duty at the precinct. In the summer of 1919, AFL granted a union charter to the Boston Social Club, the officers' fraternal organization. The police commissioner responded by issuing an order banning union membership. Leaders of the union refused to disband, and the commissioner then suspended the leaders. In September, over 1,100 of the 1,500 officer Boston police force went on strike. The city erupted in violence and eventually the governor, Calvin Coolidge, sent in the National Guard to restore order. All strikers were fired and a replacement force was hired. Boston's action in dealing with the striking officers set the tone in law enforcement toward unions that lasted for nearly fifty years (Bopp and Schultz, 1972). The labor movement in policing was dead. The message was clear - striking officers would be fired. It was not until the 1950s and the 1960s that conditions were favorable for labor unions to represent law enforcement officers in collective bargaining. Today, according to Dempsey (1999: 69):

> .....nearly 75 % of all U.S. police officers are members of labor unions. About two-thirds of all the states have collective bargaining laws for public employees. In those states, the police union bargains with the locality over wages and other conditions of employment. In the states that do not have collective bargaining agreements, the police union serves a more informal role.

There are a number of national, state and local unions. The International Association of Correctional Officers (IACO), the International Brotherhood of Correctional Officers (IBCO), and the AFSCME (American Federation of State, County and Municipal Employees) are the largest unions for correctional officers (Josi & Sechrest, 1998). All are affiliated with the ALF-CIO. Other national organizations include the National Union of Law Enforcement Associations

(NULEA) and the National Association of Police Organizations (NAPO). The California Correctional Peace Officers Association (CCPOA) is one of the largest state-level unions in the country. Founded in 1957, it represents more than 23,000 officers (ccpa.org, n/d). Since the passage of the Dills Act of 1982, which allowed collective bargaining for state employees, the CCPOA has represented state correctional officers in contract negotiations.

DiIulio (1987: 122) in examining the Michigan, California, and Texas correctional systems, states that Michigan with its long history of labor unions "has long had some of the nation's most active, powerful and militant correctional officer unions."

Jacobs (1977: 188-189), in his study of the Stateville Prison in Illinois, reported that "in the mid-1950s an educational administrator tried to organize a union around the issues of low pay, a six day work week, and summary suspensions. This effort, like others that followed, failed to attract more than a dozen employees. At no time would Joe Ragen (the warden) meet with organized groups of employees or inmates".

> In 1962 Charles Vaught, a line officer at the Joliet Prison and a former member of the UAW, began distributing newsletters and leaflets at the trailer court arguing the need for employee organization. His efforts, however, were stymied by Ragen, who had the known organizers transferred to different shifts and to the towers and other remote assignments ..... That the union was ultimately extended recognition in late 1966 can be attributed to the continued energies of its leaders, the retirement of Ragen from the Department of Public Safety, and the assistance of outside professional union organizers from AFSCME (Jacobs, 1977: 189).

The 1960s and the 1970s were turbulent times for the CO force at Stateville and other Illinois prisons. Changes in polices on how inmates were treated drove officers to join the union. In 1966 organizers from American

Federation of State, County and Municipal Employees (AFSCME) helped COs draw up by-laws and a charter, and Local 1866 of the AFSCME was formed. When several guards were injured in an incident at Stateville in 1971, coupled with the death of an officer in 1973 and other instances of escalated violence against officers, the union brought up the need for more stringent security. Better equipment, shakedowns, and more lock downs were rallying points of the union. Officer safety became paramount.

Formulation of unions or associations resulted from issues such as low pay, poor benefits, dismal working conditions, lack of equipment, inadequate training and a host of other issues. California's CO association became a strong union which contributed over one-half million dollars to help re-elect California's governor in 1994, whereas the union had spent almost a million dollars to get him elected in 1990 (Josi & Sechrest, 1998). Unions help defend members in job-related actions before government hearing bodies as well as working with legislators to passing legislation which benefits union members. According to Josi & Sechrest, (1998: 161) "the CCPOA lists 23 separate member benefits."

Not all correctional officers who are union members belong to national organizations. One of the many local unions is the Massachusetts Corrections Officers Federated Union (MCOFU) founded in 1988. Several officers who were members of the AFSCME "were fed up with the lack of support and representation by the former union" (MCOFU, n.d.). This union is made up of state correctional officers, county jail and house of corrections officers, and communication officers. Not all correctional officers in Massachusetts belong to the MCOFU. Other unions are trying to sway members to abandon the MCOFU and to join those affiliated with the IBCO. As a result the MCOFU, leadership is mounting a campaign to retain its members (see www.mcofu.com for current newsletters).

There are hundreds of associations, local, state and national unions to represent correctional and law enforcement officers throughout the country. Managers at all levels of government must work with local union or association representatives on a myriad of different issues. Each side must balance the needs of the employees in areas of salaries, benefits, training, job security, personal security and career advancement within limited budgets.

Private Prisons

With mandatory sentences, truth in sentencing and longer prison terms the number of incarcerated offenders continue to rise. Between 1925 and 1980, the inmate population averaged from a low of 79 inmates per 100,000 population to a high of 137 inmates per 100,000 population. For over 50 years there was little fluctuation in the incarceration rate. Through the 1980s and 1990s the rate grew steadily. By 1999, the incarceration rate was 468 per 100,000 population, almost a four-fold increase since 1980 (Sourcebook, 2000). In 1925, there were over 91,000 prisoners in state and federal prisons. By 1980, that number rose to over 315,000 and by 1999 the number had reached 1.2 million (Sourcebook, 2000). By the end of June 2002, the number of inmates in state and federal prisons and local jails had reached over 2 million (Beck, Karberg & Harrison, 2003). The increases in inmate populations stretched prison capacity beyond its limits. Many state systems faced overcrowding problems and state expenditures for correctional activities more than doubled from $12.7 billion in 1985 to $27.3 billion in 1996 (Stephan, 1999).

In the 1980s private sector correctional firms claimed they could save taxpayers' money in two major areas. First, they could build prisons faster and cheaper than the government and second, they could operate facilities cheaper and more efficiently than the state (Austin & Coventry, 2001). Research indicates that private companies can add to or build new prisons quicker and for less money than the government (Austin & Coventry, 2001). The focus is on how the private sector can lower operating costs. Since over two-thirds of the operating costs of a prison goes to salaries and benefits this is the area where private organizations save money. Three ways to control labor costs are to: reduce the number of staff, cut wages, and reduce fringe benefits. According to Austin and Coventry (2001: 16) "private firms claim that they can save 10 to 20 percent in prison operations due largely to efficient handling of labor costs."

Privatization is defined by Austin and Coventry (2001: 2) as "a contract process that shifts public functions, responsibilities, and capital assets, in whole or in part, from the public sector to the private sector." Privatization can range from private companies providing limited services to a government facility, such as a private company contracted to provide all medical services to the facility, whereas the same company or another company may be contracted to provide food services for the facility for the contract period. The government maintains control of all other operations of the facility. At the other end of the spectrum is where a private company provides all the services for a facility. In some instances a private company builds, operates and maintains the facility. In other instances private companies take over former government facilities.

The growth of privatization of corrections in the 1980s started slowly. World-wide, the number of inmates in private facilities in 1987 was slightly more than 3,000. By the end of 1998, that number had increased to over 130,000, of which 116,626 were in the United States. By the end of 1998, fourteen firms operated 158 facilities in 30 states. Almost one-fourth of Texas' correctional facilities are operated by private firms. Most private facilities are located in southern or western states. The top 3 states are: Texas (43), California (24) and Florida (10). Of the fourteen private correctional firms operating in 1998, two companies accounted for more than 75 percent of the world market: Corrections

Corporation of America (51.4%) and Wackenhut Corrections Corporation (25.1%). Even with the rapid growth of private facilities they still account for less than 7 percent of the U.S. market (Austin & Coventry, 2001).

The question of whether private sector correctional operations save money when compared to state-run operations has been examined in a number of different studies. In the mid-1990s, the Federal Bureau of Prisons (BOP) proposed to increase the use of private sector operations within the BOP. The bureau wanted to use private firms to operate most future pretrial detention facilities and many of the proposed minimum and low security facilities (GAO Private and Public Prisons, 1996). In its 1997 budget the Justice Department planned for the activation of two private facilities. The Justice Department, however, reversed this plan citing labor disputes with BOP employees. The private sector continued to claim cost savings over government operations. Eventually the GAO, the investigative branch of the U.S. Congress, initiated a review to: (1) identify studies which compared operational costs and/ or the quality of service of private and public correctional facilities; (2) determine what could be concluded regarding costs and/or quality of service; (3) assess whether the results could be generalized to other corrections systems; and (4) identify lessons learned to guide future research. The GAO selected five studies conducted in the 1990s comparing private and public facilities. Based on their evaluation of studies conducted in California, Tennessee, Washington, Texas, and New Mexico for state and federal prisons, the GAO report stated "we could not conclude from these studies that privatization ..... will not save money. However, these studies do not offer substantial evidence that savings have occurred" (GAO Private and Public Prisons, 1996: 4). This report further concluded that "these studies offer little generalizable guidance for other jurisdictions about what to expect regarding comparative operational costs and quality of service if they were to move toward privatizing correctional facilities" (GAO Private and Public Prisons, 1996: 4).

Two of the studies showed no significant differences in operating costs between public and private facilities, one study reported a seven percent difference for the private facility, while another study reported one private facility to be more costly than one public facility but less costly than another. The fifth study reported up to a 15 percent savings for private facility. It compared a functioning private facility with a hypothetical public facility rather than comparing the private facility with an existing state facility. Because of the varying results the GAO "could not conclude whether privatization saved money" (GAO Private and Public Prisons, 1996: 4).

Austin and Coventry's (2001) monograph on emerging issues in privatized prisons devote one full chapter to research regarding privatization. Their report was more comprehensive than the 1996 GAO report. The authors reviewed eight different studies from across the country. They concluded:

> ....the cost benefits of privatization have not materialized to the extent promised by the private sector. Although there are examples of cost savings, there are other examples in which such benefits have not been realized. Moreover, it is probably too early to determine if the initial cost savings can be sustained over a long time period. It only takes one major disturbance for such costs to greatly accelerate (Austin and Coventry, 2001: 29).

One major criticism of these research projects was that these studies were "essentially one-time studies that measure the attributes of private and public facilities at a given time" (Austin and Coventry, 2001: 37). Continuing questions are, can private facilities sustain cost savings over extended periods of time? Would these savings continue to hold true if staff salaries and fringe benefits increase with length of service as it does for public employees? Since about 80 percent of a public agency's budget is for salaries and benefits, it will take time for private facilities to reach the level of employee costs currently borne by the state.

Infectious Diseases

Correctional officers can be exposed to a variety of infectious diseases. More than 25 diseases are spread primarily through sexual activities. It is estimated there are more than 65 million Americans living with an incurable sexually transmitted disease. Annually, more than 15 million people become infected, and about half will have life-long infections (CDC Tracking the Hidden Epidemics, 2000). HIV and hepatitis B are bloodborne pathogens contracted by exposure to infectious blood or body fluids. Sexual activities and sharing needles or syringes are common methods of spreading these two diseases. There are no recorded cases of a correctional officer contracting HIV from exposure to an inmate. Tuberculosis (TB) is an airborne disease. It occurs when an infected person coughs or sneezes and a non-infected person breathes in the contaminated air. Although rare, precautions must be taken by correctional officers when dealing with inmates with TB. The following sections examine major infectious diseases prevalent in a prison setting that may endanger correctional officers.

Sexually transmitted diseases include common diseases as HIV, gonorrhea, genital warts, herpes, syphilis, vaginitis, and yeast infections. If left untreated all can become serious medical problems. Some are treatable with antibiotics and others, such as HIV, and herpes, can be controlled with other medications. Few correctional systems require mandatory testing of inmates for all types of STDs. About 90 percent of federal and state systems have mandatory or routine screening for syphilis. Fewer have screening for gonorrhea or chlamydia. According to Hammett and Harmon (1999: 21), "the most striking point about these survey findings is the rarity of screening and the paucity of screening data." They go on to conclude that "although available data are incomplete, it appears that rates of STDs ..... are higher among inmates than in the overall population" (Hammett & Harman, 1999: 22). The only way a correctional officer can contract

STDs from an inmate is to have sex with an infected inmate. Screening and prevention are the most effective ways to reduce STDs in prison. Educational programs for officers in their basic academy and annual in-service educational programs inform officers as to the risks. Educational programs and behavior intervention programs are provided by institution for inmates.

In 2003, more than 38 million people worldwide were infected with the HIV virus. More than 20 million have died since it was first identified in 1981 (UNAIDS, 2004). In the United States almost one million people have HIV, with 40,000 new cases each year. About one quarter are unaware they are infected. It is growing most among minorities and is a leading cause of death for 25 - 44 year-old black males (NIAID, 2003). More than 16,000 died from this disease in the United States in 2002. At the end of 2001, almost 25,000 state and federal inmates where known be HIV positive. These inmates account for about 2 percent of state and 1.2 percent of federal inmates. The rate of confirmed cases in state and federal custody is about three times that of the general population. The good news is that AIDS-related deaths of inmates have declined substantially in recent years (Maruschak, 2004). Yet inmates account of only .7% of the general population (CDC, 2003). High risk behaviors of inmates such as sex, drug use, sharing of injection materials, and tattooing, increase the risk of infection. Table 9.1 provides data for each state and the federal prison system for the number of inmates with HIV and the percentage of HIV positive inmates to the general prison population. New York, Florida, and California lead the nation with the largest number of HIV inmates. In the last ten years the number of infected inmates increased, stabilized and in most states started decreasing. Louisiana experienced the largest growth going from 0.7 percent in 1991 to 2.6 percent of the prison population infected with HIV in 2001. New York experienced the largest drop, falling from 13. 8 percent in 1991 to 8.1 percent in 2001.

TABLE 9.1
INMATES HIV POSITIVE 2001

State	Total Known	Percentage	State	Total Known	Percentage
Alabama	302	1.2	Nebraska	24	0.6
Alaska	16	0.5	Nevada	127	1.4
Arizona	122	0.4	New Hampshire	17	0.7
Arkansas	108	0.9	New Jersey	804	3.4
California	1,305	0.8	New Mexico	27	0.5
Colorado	173	1.2	New York	5,500	8.1
Connecticut	604	3.5	North Carolina	573	1.8
Delaware	143	2.1	North Dakota	4	0.4
D.C.	NA	NA	Ohio	398	0.9
Florida	2,602	3.6	Oklahoma	573	1.8
Georgia	1,150	2.5	Oregon	30	0.3
Idaho	14	0.4	Pennsylvania	735	2.0
Illinois	593	1.3	Rhode Island	148	4.4
Indiana	NA	NA	South Carolina	559	2.6
Iowa	27	0.3	South Dakota	5	0.2
Kansas	41	0.5	Tennessee	231	1.7
Kentucky	105	1.1	Texas	2,388	1.8
Louisiana	514	2.6	Utah	34	0.8
Maine	15	0.9	Vermont	NA	NA
Maryland	830	2.0	Virginia	507	1.7
Massachusetts	307	3.0	Washington	88	0.6
Michigan	584	1.2	West Virginia	16	0.5
Minnesota	33	0.5	Wisconsin	164	0.9
Mississippi	234	2.0	Wyoming	4	0.4
Missouri	262	0.9	Federal	1,520	1.2
Montana	11	0.6			

Source: Table compiled from *HIV in Prisons and Jails, 1993*; *HIV in Prison and Jails, 1996*; and *HIV in Prisons and Jails, 2001*.

AIDS - acquired immunodeficiency syndrome - is caused by the human immunodeficiency virus (HIV) which progressively destroys the body's ability to fight to fight infections. There are three common ways for HIV to pass from one person to another: by having unprotected sex (semen or vaginal fluids), by sharing contaminated needles or syringes (blood), and from mother to child (before or during child birth or through breast feeding). There is no scientific evidence that HIV is spread through sweat, tears, urine or feces. HIV cannot be contracted through the air, when someone coughs or sneezes, as it is not an airborne pathogen. It cannot be contracted by touching or shaking hands with an infected person. Infection is not possible from a toilet seat, telephone, water fountain, or sharing a drinking glass, food plate or utensils (Treathiv.com, n.d.). It has also been reported that HIV cannot be contracted from closed mouth or social kissing (there is one reported case involving French kissing). According to NIAID (2003: 1), "it is rare for a patient to give HIV to a health care worker or vice - versa by accidental sticks with contaminated needles or other medical instruments." There are no known cases where a correctional officers has contracted the HIV virus as a result of contact with an infected inmate. Education, testing and behavioral interventions are keys to reducing the risks. Basic correctional officer training academies provide training on physical and mental health which would include sections on infectious diseases. This training continues once an officer is on the job. The Wisconsin Department of Corrections, for example, provides 4 hours of annual in-service training on issues relating to infectious diseases. Correctional departments may require newly hired officers to take a HIV test. For inmates there are three board categories of testing policies: mandatory, routine and voluntary. Of the 50 states and the Federal Bureau of Prisons, the most common reasons for testing are *upon inmate request* (46 jurisdictions), *upon clinical indication of need* (46 jurisdictions), *court order* (43 jurisdictions), *upon involvement in an incident* (41 jurisdictions), *all in-coming inmates* (19 jurisdictions), *high-risk groups* (15 jurisdictions), *all inmates currently in custody* (5 jurisdictions), *random sample* (4 jurisdictions), and *all inmates prior to release* (4 jurisdictions)(Bureau of Justice Statistics, 2000).

Information about an inmate's HIV status is protected information and correctional officers are not informed as to which inmates are HIV positive. But nothing prevents an inmate from informing an officer of that inmate's health, and, since many times it is the correctional officer who distributes medication to inmates, it would not take the officer long to figure out who is getting what type of medications. Some correctional facilities may isolate HIV infected inmates in separate areas. Alabama, for example, confines all HIV inmates at the Limestone Correctional Facility in Capshaw, Alabama. More than 200 inmates are housed in a converted warehouse in the Special Unit section of the prison. Several other states also segregate HIV inmates. Inmate groups have challenged the segregation policies but, so far, the courts have sided with correctional institutions and continue to allow facilities to segregate infected inmates (Anonymous, 2003; Crary, 2001).

Inmates have a legal right to health care and cannot be denied treatment for HIV/AIDS. Medical treatment is an Eighth Amendment issue and the Supreme Court has held that deliberate indifference to serious medical needs is prohibited. Correctional officers cannot deny or delay access to medical care nor deny reception of medical treatment, including medicines, to inmates.

Educating correctional officers and inmates about HIV is one method correctional institutions can use to reduce or prevent the spread of HIV and other infectious diseases. These programs usually include written materials, audiovisual materials, counseling sessions, and peer or instructor-led education programs. The majority of state and federal institutions offer a variety of educational programs (Hammett and Harmon, 1999). In order to reduce the high risk behaviors for HIV transmission in a correctional setting, correctional officials could make available condoms for distribution to inmates, provide bleach as a disinfection for needles and syringes, and provide needle and syringe exchanges. Consensual and coercive sex occurs in the prison setting and providing condoms, while not condoning this behavior, can reduce the risk of spreading disease. Bleach in full strength can be used as a disinfectant for needles and syringes for drug use or in tattooing. Needle and syringe exchange programs, while not in use in this country because of laws or correctional regulations that prohibit the possession of these items, are being used successfully in other countries (Hammett and Harmon, 1999b). These procedures would decrease the likelihood of spreading the disease through contaminated needles and syringes.

Hepatitis is a virus disease which damages the liver. If left untreated it can cause death. There are five types of viral hepatitis. Hepatitis A, B and C are the most common forms. The most frequent method of spreading Hepatitis A is through close personal contact (household contact, sexual contact, or drug use). Household or sexual contact is the most frequent source of infection followed by injection drug use. There are no long-term effects of this disease and once a person has hepatitis A he/she can not get it again. There is a vaccination available. Fortunately there have been no reported outbreaks of hepatitis A in correctional institutions. It is a concern in correctional settings because of the high-risk behavior of inmates. In correctional settings, men having sex with men (MSM) and injection drug users are the at-risk groups (Weinbaum et al., 2003).

Hepatitis B is a bloodborne pathogen which occurs when blood or bodily fluids (semen or saliva) from an infect person enter the body of a non - immune person. Unprotected sex with multiple partners is the predominant way this disease spreads in a correctional setting. The second means of spreading this disease is in sharing needles or syringes for injection drug use. Vaccination is the best prevention against hepatitis B. Correctional officers and inmates receive a 3 shoot series spread out over a 6 month period. The prevalence rate for hepatitis

B, 12.5 percent for correctional officers, is similar to that of the general population. For inmates it ranges from 13 percent to 47 percent depending upon the region of the country. Women inmates have a higher prevalence rate than male inmates, and for inmates with chronic HBV (hepatitis B virus) the rate is 2 - 6 times higher than the rate of the general population. Hepatitis B is more of a concern among inmates than correctional officers. Vaccination of inmates and staff is the best strategy to prevent HBV infections.

Hepatitis C Virus (HCV) is a bloodborne pathogen transmitted by direct exposure to infectious blood. Most commonly spread by the sharing of needles and syringes, it is more prevalent among drug users than any other group. About 1.8 percent of the United States population is infected with HCV while about 1.3 percent are chronically infected. The infection rate is much higher for inmates. Estimates range from about 12 percent to a high of 35 percent who have chronic HCV infection. "HCV infection is primarily associated with a history of injection - drug use" (Weinbaum et al., 2003: 7). Currently, there are no published reports on the prevalence rate among correctional officers. At the present time no vaccine exists to prevent HCV infection, therefore prevention is the best strategy to reduce the transmission of this disease. Medical screening at correctional intake, and inmate education, are the best methods. As mentioned in the above section on AIDS, trying to reduce the high-risk behaviors (unprotected sex, sharing of needles) is paramount for correctional officials. Most state and federal facilities vaccinate inmates for hepatitis B, test for HBV and HCV, and provide educational and counseling sessions. Correctional officers receive hepatitis B vaccinations as well as ongoing education and training concerning supervising inmates with hepatitis infections.

Tuberculosis (TB) is an airborne disease spread when an infected person coughs or sneezes. It mainly affects the lungs but can affect the brain, kidneys or the spine. When a healthy person inhales air containing TB germs, he/she may become infected. Individuals with TB infection (latent TB infection) do not feel sick or display any symptoms. They can not infect others, but may at some later time develop the disease. In only about 10 percent of the cases in which a person is infected will the infection progress to the disease. If left untreated the infection will progress to the disease stage in a manner of a few weeks. Symptoms of TB include feeling sick or weak, weight loss, fever and night sweats. Symptoms of TB in the lungs include coughing, chest pain and coughing up blood (Centers for Disease Control and Prevention, 1999).

Correctional officers may be at risk of contracting either the infection or the disease depending on what control measures are in place. There has been one confirmed death of a correctional officer who died during a 1991 outbreak of multi-drug resistant TB in New York state (Hammett, and Harmon, 1999b). In 2002, inmates infected with TB represented about 3.1 percent of all inmates nationwide. Arizona, with 7.3%, lead the way followed by Texas (7%), Georgia (5.2%) and Florida (5%) (CDC, 2003b). Many inmates with TB are also co-infected with HIV. In 1996, CDC (Centers for Disease Control and Prevention) revised guidelines for the prevention and control of TB in Correctional facilities. These guidelines focused on three areas of activities: screening, containment and assessment (U.S. Department of Health & Human Services, 1995). The CDC recommended all inmates receive the PPD skin test at intake and on an annual basis. Correctional officers should have the PPD skin test at hiring and at annual intervals. Screening is seen as the first line of defense. Containment includes preventing transmission and providing adequate treatment, which includes isolating an inmate from the general population. Assessment includes monitoring and evaluating screening and containment efforts (Hammett, and Harmon, 1999c).

If a new inmate tests positive for TB at the Reception Center he/she is immediately placed in isolation. In the Oklahoma system inmates are placed in an airborne infection isolation room (AIIR). Inmates with suspected or confirmed cases of TB are removed from the general population and placed in AIIR rooms either on site or at another facility until no longer infectious, which is between 3 - 4 weeks. Inmates are tested at reception and annually thereafter. For new employees in Oklahoma, TB testing is mandatory, and annual testing is at the discretion of medical services leaders (Oklahoma DOC Tuberculosis Control Program, 2000).

Tuberculosis is curable, with treatment regimens and lengths of treatment varying depending upon early detection. Infected persons are given a variety of drugs for up to six months or longer. Directly observed therapy (DOT), in which the patient is observed taking each dose of medicines, is the most successful method to insure patients are complying with a recommended treatment program. Inmates with HIV related tuberculosis may receive treatment for years.

Violence and the Use of Force

Prisons and jails can be dangerous places for inmates and officers alike. In 2000 there were almost 18,000 inmate assaults on staff members in state and federal prisons for a rate of 14.6 per 1,000 inmates. Five staff members lost their lives in 2000. These numbers are down considerably from 1995 when there were 14 deaths and over 24,000 assaults (Bureau of Justice Statistics, 2003). In 2000, there were 34,355 assaults on inmates resulting in 51 inmate deaths (Stephan and Karberg, 2003). In our nation's jails there were over 9,000 inmate assaults on employees, or a rate of 17.8 per 1,000. Four jail staff members lost their lives in 1999 (Stephan, 2001). While the number of inmate assaults is unknown there were 919 inmate deaths in 1999. Over half of the deaths were the result of disease or natural causes. Over a third of inmate deaths were suicides. Only 28, or 3 percent of jail inmate deaths were the result of homicides. A detailed examination of inmate assaults in 2002 is provided in Table 9.2.

Correctional officers have the legal authority to use force up to and including deadly force. According to the Oklahoma Department of Corrections, the use of force is defined as "any action which involves physical contact in a confrontational situation which is employed by staff using authorized means to obtain compliance by inmates/offenders with orders from staff, to control disruptive/ violent inmates, enforce or restore order to a prison facility, protect persons from imminent death or serious bodily harm, to protect state property, prevent escapes, and capture escaped inmates" (Oklahoma Department of Corrections, 2003)

There are two appropriate levels of force which a correctional officer may use. These are non-deadly force and deadly force. Oklahoma's DOC (2003) defines non-deadly force as "the use of any physical force, with a device other than a firearm, against a human being, which was designed either for defensive purposes or to temporarily incapacitate, immobilize, or disorient a person." Correctional officers have a wide range of equipment at their disposal including: physical restraint devices such as handcuffs, leg irons, straight jackets and restraint chairs; chemical/ inflammatory agents such as tear gas or pepper spray; electronic technology such as Taser stun guns and electronic shields, water under high pressure used to disorient an inmate, stun guns that launch bean bags, and batons or similar weapons. This equipment is designed to immobilize, incapacitate or disorient inmates long enough for correctional officers to regain control of a situation. The Wisconsin Department of Correction states force "means the exercise of strength or power to overcome resistance or to compel another to act or to refrain from acting in a particular way" (DOC 306.02 (10)).

TABLE 9.2
ASSAULTS COMMITTED BY INMATES
2002

State	Against Staff	Against Inmates	State	Against Staff	Against Inmates
Alabama			Nebraska	178	243
Alaska		134	Nevada	20	
Arizona	258	773	New Hampshire	20	
Arkansas	198	445	New Jersey	182	426
California	2,813	4,397	New Mexico	155	164
Colorado	449	694	New York	683	843
Connecticut	323	1,008	North Carolina	118	513
Delaware	67	129	North Dakota	118	513
D.C.	35	84	Ohio	528	445
Florida	587	1,944	Oklahoma	154	877
Georgia	703	1,142	Oregon	130	413
Idaho	24	134	Pennsylvania	24	24
Illinois	878	2,058	Rhode Island	30	28
Indiana	706	925	South Carolina	561	272
Iowa	121	176	South Dakota	47	56
Kansas	234	143	Tennessee	2	840
Kentucky	4	62	Texas	61	673
Louisiana	577	2,252	Utah	23	150
Maine	50	152	Vermont		173
Maryland	127	1,383	Virginia	20	65
Massachusetts	296		Washington	78	848
Michigan	328	473	West Virginia	85	89
Minnesota	71	259	Wisconsin	714	437
Mississippi	368	339	Wyoming	10	20
Missouri	3,291	1,602			
Montana	9	63	total	16,435	28,827

Source: Camp, C. (2003). *The Corrections Yearbook 2002.* Middleton, CT: Criminal Justice Institute, Inc.

202

Non-deadly force may be used against inmates "only if the user of force reasonably believes it is immediately necessary to realize one of the following purposes:

A. To prevent death or bodily injury to oneself or another.
B. To regain control of an institution or part of an institution.
C. To prevent escape or apprehend an escapee.
D. To change the location of an inmate.
E. To control a disruptive inmate.
F. To prevent unlawful damage to property.
G. To enforce a departmental rule, a policy or procedure or an order of a staff member (DOC 306.07 (2)).

Correctional officers can use force in the course of their duties to ensure compliance of orders and to maintain discipline. The Supreme Court has held that the use of force by correctional officers in good faith to maintain or restore discipline is constitutional. The use of excessive force, however, is not constitutional. If force is applied maliciously and sadistically to cause harm, the Court has held this to be cruel and unusual punishment in violation of the Eight Amendment. In *Hudson v. McMillian et al* (1992), a case in which a correctional officer, after arguing with an inmate, repeatedly punched the inmate while at the same time a second officer held the inmate in place and repeatedly punched and kicked the inmate. Another officer, who was the supervisor, watched the beating but merely told the other officers "not to have too much fun". In this case the Court held that the officers' actions amounted to excessive force, and therefore constituted cruel and unusual punishment. In another case, the handcuffing of an inmate by correctional officers to a hitching post on two different occasions as punishment, the first time for two hours and the second time for seven hours, amounted to cruel and unusual punishment. The Court, in *Hope v Pelzer et al* (2002), held that this type of punitive treatment amounted to the gratuitous infliction of wanton and unnecessary pain. However, in both of these cases the Court did not prohibit the use of force, but only the *unnecessary* use of force.

According to Oklahoma Department of Corrections (2003) "use of force standards", correctional officers have the right to use deadly force, which is force that is likely to cause death or serious bodily injury. In general, correctional officers may use deadly force: to prevent an escape from a prison by an inmate or during transportation of an inmate who has been convicted of a felony; or when a staff member reasonably believes it is necessary to protect himself/herself or others from the imminent infliction of death or serious bodily harm; or to maintain or restore control of a prison when staff reasonably believes the intended subject of deadly force is participating in a disturbance in a manner that threatens the safety of the physical plant. In other words, a correctional officer may use deadly force to prevent an escape, to protect oneself or others, or to prevent damage to the prison. The Wisconsin Department of Corrections deadly force policy is slightly different. Like Oklahoma, Wisconsin correctional officers can use deadly force to prevent an escape, or to apprehend an escaped inmate, to protect himself/ herself or others from imminent death or serious bodily injury, or to regain control of the whole institution or part on an institution. There is, however, a difference with Oklahoma law. In Wisconsin, deadly force is authorized when there is unlawful damage to property *that may result in death or serious injury*. While there are differences, each state has developed policies and procedures governing the use of force. The American Correctional Association has established standards for adult correctional institutions and states can model their policies and procedures after the ACA standards.

The United States Supreme Court has addressed the issue of use of deadly force in correctional settings. In *Whitely v. Albers* (1986), a case involving correctional officers shooting an inmate while restoring order in a prison after a correctional officer was taken hostage. This case was decided under the Eight Amendment. The case hinged on whether or not the shooting was a good faith effort to restore discipline, or whether the action by the correctional officer was malicious or sadistic with the purpose of causing harm to the inmate. If the former was true then there was no violation of the cruel and unusual punishment clause of the Eight Amendment. If the latter was true then the officer's action (shooting the inmate in the leg with a shotgun) would constitute cruel and unusual punishment. The Court held that the actions of the officer were applied in good faith and the use of deadly force is a legitimate means of restoring order in a correctional setting.

Emergency Response Teams

All correctional officers receive basic firearms training in the academy and on the job. There are times, however, when specialized response teams are needed to maintain or to regain control of a situation in a correctional institution. In 2000, there were 606 major disturbances at state facilities. These were disturbances where numerous inmates were involved which resulted in serious injury or significant property damage (Stephan and Karberg, 2003). The Federal Bureau of Prisons' special operations and response teams (SORT) date back to the 1980s in response to riots at several federal prisons. Currently the BOP has 44 SORTs with over 700 officers to provide emergency responses to 100 institutions nationwide. Members are highly trained in a variety of tasks in responding to prison disturbances or in supporting local law enforce during civil unrest or natural disasters. The Bureau of Prisons also has at each institution Disturbance Control Teams and these provide the primary institutional response to a situation until the

SORT arrives, or they can complement a SORT if needed. Many federal institutions also have Hostage Negotiation Teams to provide support in case of hostage situations (specialoperations.com, n.d.).

State correctional organizations and local jails have similar types of response teams. Correctional Emergency Response Teams (CERT) vary in size and functions, depending upon the needs of each organization. In 1982, the Connecticut Department of Corrections (CTDOC) formed a 30 man CERT for the state. Since then the unit has gone on to become the Special Operations Unit which has two CERT teams, the Special Operation Group (SOG) hostage rescue team, Situational Control (SITCON) Hostage Negotiation Team, Canine unit (with 20 teams), and an Armory operations and Firearms Training Unit. The SOG is commanded by a major who is the Chief of Tactical Operations. All members of the unit continually train with current equipment and updated tactics (specwarnet.com, n.d.). Local jails may also have emergency response teams. As the largest municipal jail in Kentucky, the Jefferson County Metropolitan Corrections Department established its first 20 man CERT team in 1984. Today, over 50 officers and command staff make up the CERT unit with 24 hour coverage (Colvin, n.d.).

One of the primary functions of a CERT is cell extraction, the forceful removal of a non-compliant inmate from a cell or other location. The number of team members may vary but generally it is a 5 officer team. The goal of a cell extraction team is to get an individual out safely without injury to the inmate or officers. This can hopefully be accomplished through voluntary compliance on the part of the inmate. Imagine the intimidating aspect projected by 5 officers dressed in Battle Dress Uniforms (BDUs) with full body protection (extraction shield, helmet with face shield, protective vest, gas mask, gloves, groin protectors, elbow and knee pads, handcuffs/ flexcuffs, OC spray and baton), preparing to charge into a cell. For an inmate who refuses to comply with the movement order the extraction team will forcibly remove the inmate. While not part of the extraction team, a video camera operator records the entire extraction process and medical staff are present to provide treatment if necessary (Topham, n.d.).

The Professionalization of Correctional Officers

To cope with the ever-changing problems encountered in the operation of modern correctional facilities and their diverse inmate populations, it has become necessary for correctional officers themselves to continually adapt and change. One process that has been implemented to increase the skills of COs is *professionalization.* Champion (2005: 206-207) defines professionalization as "the process of acquiring standards, greater education, practical skill, certification, and recognition from approved bodies, which promotes more ethical behavior and a commitment to excellent community service and quality of life." Key points of this definition include 1) developing standards, 2) acquiring an education and expertise, and 3) obtaining some type of certification from a recognized body. As indicated below, it has been a long road to get to the level of professionalization that is evident in the field of corrections today.

Films like *The Shawshanke Redemption, ConAir* and *Cool Hand Luke* have long portrayed correction officers as corrupt, violent, and uneducated. As was pointed out earlier in this text, in the past correctional officers had little if any training, worked long hours for little pay, and political patronage was the main qualification of the job. Corrections was seen as an occupational field, one requiring little skill. It was a just a job for many, a steady paycheck for others, and a job with security for still others. Corrections had an image problem. In response to criticism in the 1967 President's Task Force Report, correctional organizations had, by the 1970s, begun instituting minimal standards and training.

Education and training were seen as the two key components for the professionalization of correctional officers. Also during this time frame a philosophical shift occurred, away from officers being merely security officers more toward becoming a part of the rehabilitation process. Correctional officers were seen as human service-oriented professionals, able to help in the rehabilitation of offenders (Pollock, 1997). The move to professionalize administrators was underway as well. In Illinois, for example, prior to the 1970s none of the wardens had college degree. By 1974, 75% of all wardens in the state had master's degrees. For correctional officers, the minimal education requirement for all department of corrections reviewed for this research is a high school diploma or GED, which is similar for most law enforcement careers. Some, like the Federal Bureau of Prisons, require a bachelor's degree or three years of work experience.

The proliferation of criminal justice educational programs aided in this transition. The number of criminal justice programs at community colleges and universities has increased from 40 institutions granting associates degrees in 1960, to over 1000 in 1990. The number of colleges and universities granting undergraduate increased from 15 to 687 and graduate degrees increased from 15 to over 150. Today about 20 universities offer doctoral degrees (Bufkin, 2004). Most criminal justice programs evolved out of police science programs. According to Dempsey and Forst (2005), in an attempt to professionalize police, Berkeley, California, police chief August Vollmer incorporated university education as part of his police officers' training. Vollmer also helped develop the School of Criminology at the University of California-Berkeley. The movement to professionalize police was further advanced with the passage of federal legislation in 1968 creating the Law Enforcement Education Program (LEEP). Millions of dollars were pumped into this program, which provided loans and grants for law enforcement officers to take college courses. Coincidentally, there was a growth of law enforcement-related programs to capitalize on all these federal monies. Many programs moved away from police academy-type courses, which were job-related types of courses, to broader-based courses in social science and liberal arts. This was a both an attempt to provide students with an education which better equipped them to deal with issues of modern urban life, and also to legitimate criminal justice as "a full fledged academic discipline" (Farnworth, Longmire and West, 1998: 41). Many criminal justice programs are therefore firmly grounded in the social sciences and liberal arts. Courtright and Makey's (2004) exploratory study of five colleges in the northeast found that most criminal justice majors want to be police officers, and federal law enforcement officers in particular. Students in their study, when rating occupations, rated "correctional related" occupations lower than law enforcement occupations.

Organizations like the American Correctional Association (ACA) have made great strides in the area of professional development for correctional officers. The ACA has instituted the Corrections Certification Program whose purpose "is to provide a national, voluntary method by which individuals can gain recognition as qualified corrections practitioners" (American Correctional Association, n.d.). While the role of the correctional officers may have yet to reach the status of a true profession, the process in well underway. Hopefully, as more prison systems attempt to achieve accreditation from organizations like the ACA, the quality of life for both inmates and COs will be enhanced.

Summary and Conclusion

The prison is a constantly changing and evolving social environment. Changes in law, in the inmate population, and in societal expectations, have all forced correctional officers to change and adapt. No longer are prisons brutal dungeons where the only function of correctional officers was to "take names and kick ass". The protection of inmate rights by the courts has changed the way officers may apply force. Yet levels of prison violence continue to be high, and new methodologies have been developed to respond to violence while protecting the welfare and rights of both inmates and officers. New infectious diseases have become common in prisons, and threaten the health of correctional officers. Correctional officers have responded to these difficulties. By unionizing and professionalizing, COs have increased the status of their occupation, and challenged the old stereotype of the "prison guard".

Correctional officers are experts in adaptation. As society changed its correctional philosophy from punishment to rehabilitation to justice, correctional officers changed too. New demands brought new responses. Educational levels increased, training levels increased, and the correctional officer corps diversified. Minorities and women were recruited, and their contributions helped prisons adapt to new inmate challenges. Correctional officers face serious psychological and physical dangers, yet they carry on. Virtually invisible, and many times misunderstood by the American public, correctional officers serve as a human shield, protecting that same public from those anti-social elements society has banished to prison. To most in America, sentencing a criminal to prison is the end of the problem. But for the correctional officer, it is just the beginning.

BIBLIOGRAPHY

Allen, H., & Simonsen, C. (1995). *Corrections in America.* Upper Saddle River, NJ: Prentice Hall.

Alpert, G. (1984). "The Needs of the Judiciary and Misapplication of Social Research: The Case of Female Guards in Men's Prisons." *Criminology* 22: 441-456.

American Correctional Association (2001). *2001 Directory of Adult and Juvenile Correctional Departments, Institutions, Agencies, and Probation and Parole Authorities* (62nd ed.). White Plains, MD: Automated Graphics.

American Correctional Association (n.d.). "Professional Certification." Retrieved September 16, 2005, from http://www.aca.org/certification/

American Probation and Parole Association (n.d.) *Adult Probation and Parole Directory.* Retrieved September 1, 2004, from http://www.appanet.org/ directory.

Anonymous (2003). "HIV Testing in Correctional Settings." *Corrections Forum* 12: 35-38, 68-69.

Archambeault, W., & Archambeault, B. (1982). *Correctional Supervisory Management: Principles of Organization, Policy, and Law.* Englewood Cliffs, NJ: Prentice-Hall.

Austin, J. & G. Coventry (2001). *Emerging Issues on Privatized Prisons.* U.S. Department of Justice. NCJ 181249.

Barnes, H. (1972). *The Story of Punishment: A Record of Man's Inhumanity to Man.* (2nd ed.). Montclair, NJ: Patterson Smith

Bartollas, C. (1981). *Introduction to Corrections.* New York: Harper and Row, Publishers.

Beck, A., Karberg, J., & Harrison, P. (2003). *Prison and Jail Inmates at Midyear 2001.* U.S. Department of Justice. NCJ -191702.

Berger, R. (1978). "Public Image of Corrections." *California Youth Authority Quarterly* 31: 2-17.

Blau, J., Light, S., & Chamlin, M. (1986). "Individual and Contextual Effects on Stress and Job Satisfaction: A Study of Prison Staff". *Work and Occupations* 13: 131-156.

Bopp, W., & Schultz, D. (1972). *A Short History of American Law Enforcement.* Springfield, IL: Charles C. Thomas Publisher.

Bowersox, M. (1981). "Women in Corrections: Competence, Competition, and the Social Responsibility Norm." *Criminal Justice and Behavior* 8: 491-499.

Broderick, J. (1977). *Police in a Time of Change.* Morristown, NJ: General Learning Press.

Brown, J., Langan, P., & Levin, D. (1999). *Felony Sentences in State Courts, 1996.* U.S. Department of Justice NCJ 173939.

Brown, R. (1996). *A History of the Fleet Prison, London: The Anatomy of the Fleet.* Lampeter, UK: The Edwin Mellen Press, Ltd.

Britton, D. (1997). "Perceptions of the Work Environment Among Correctional Officers: Do Race and Sex Matter?" *Criminology* 35: 85-105.

Bufkin, J. (2004). "Criminology/Criminal Justice Master's Programs in the United States: Searching for Commonalities." *Journal of Criminal Justice Education*, 15, 239-262.

Bureau of Justice Statistics. (2001). *Census of State and Federal Correctional Facilities, 2000.* Washington, D.C.: U.S. Department of Justice.

Bureau of Justice Statistics. (2000). *Sourcebook of Criminal Justice Statistics 1999.* Washington, D.C.: U.S. Government Printing Office.

Bureau of Justice Statistics. (2003). *Sourcebook of Criminal Justice Statistics, 2000.* Washington, DC.: U.S. Department of Justice.

Bureau of Justice Statistics. (1999). *Sourcebook of Criminal Justice Statistics, 1998.* Washington, DC.: U.S. Department of Justice.

Bureau of Justice Statistics. (1995). *Sourcebook of Criminal Justice Statistics, 1994.* Washington, DC.: U.S. Department of Justice.

Bureau of Justice Statistics. (1993). *Sourcebook of Criminal Justice Statistics, 1993.* Washington, DC.: U.S. Department of Justice.

Bureau of Justice Statistics. (1992). *Sourcebook of Criminal Justice Statistics, 1991.* Washington, DC.: U.S. Department of Justice.

Bureau of Justice Statistics. (1991). *Sourcebook of Criminal Justice Statistics, 1990.* Washington, DC.: U.S. Department of Justice.

Bureau of Justice Statistics. (1990). *Sourcebook of Criminal Justice Statistics, 1989.* Washington, DC.: U.S. Department of Justice.

Bureau of Justice Statistics. (1989). *Sourcebook of Criminal Justice Statistics, 1988.* Washington, DC.: U.S. Department of Justice.

Bureau of Justice Statistics. (1988). *Sourcebook of Criminal Justice Statistics, 1985.* Washington, DC.: U.S. Department of Justice.

Bureau of Prisons (n.d.). "Job Information: Correctional Officer." Retrieved January 10, 2003, from http://www.bop.gov/hrmpg/hrmcorrectional officer.html

Burton, V., Ju, X., Dunaway, R., & Wolfe, N. (1991). "The Correctional Orientation of Bermuda Prison Guards: An Assessment of Attitudes toward Punishment and Rehabilitation. *International Journal of Comparative and Applied Criminal Justice* 15: 113-125.

Camp, C. (Ed) (2003). *Corrections Yearbook 2002.* Middletown, CT: Criminal Justice Institute.

Camp, C. (Ed) (2002). *Corrections Yearbook 2001.* Middletown, CT: Criminal Justice Institute.

California Department of Corrections. (n.d.). "Stand Out." Retrieved April 5, 2002, from http://cdc.state.ca.us/Inside/recruit/recruit1.htm

California Correctional Peace Officers Association. (n.d.). *History of CCPOA.* Retrieved April 22, 2003, from http://www.ccpoa.org.

Carroll, L. (1988). *Hacks, Blacks, and Cons: Race Relations in a Maximum Security Prison.* Prospects Heights, IL: Waveland Press.

Carroll, L. (1980). "The Frustrated Hacks". In B. Crouch (Ed.), *The Keepers.* Springfield: Charles Thomas Publishers.

Centers for Disease Control and Prevention. (2003b). "Reported Tuberculosis in the United States, 2002." Retrieved August 5, 2004, from http://www. cdc.gov/nchstp/tb/surv/surv2002/default.htm.

Centers for Disease Control and Prevention. (2001). "Tracking the Hidden Epidemics: Trends in STDs in the United States, 2000." Retrieved August 17, 2004, from http://www.cdc.gov/nchstp/dstd/Stats/Trends/ Trends2000.pdf

Centers for Disease Control and Prevention. (1999). "Tuberculosis Information-Tuberculosis: General Information." Retrieved August 3, 2004, from http://www.cdc.gov/nchstp/tb/pubs/tbfactsheets/250010.pdf

Chang, D., Iacovetta, R., & Janeksela, G. (1990). "A Comparison of Korean and American Security Officers' Perceptual Evaluation of Prison Inmates and Other Significant Status Groups." *International Review of Modern Sociology* 20: 113-126.

Champion, D.J. (2005). *The American Dictionary of Criminal Justice: Key Terms and Major Court Cases* (3rd). Los Angeles: Roxbury Publishing Company.

Champion, D.J. (2005). *Probation, Parole, and Community Corrections* (5th). Upper Saddle River, NJ: Prentice-Hall.

Chapman, J., Minor, E., Rieker, P., Mills,T., & Bottum, M. (1983). *Women Employed in Corrections.* Washington, D.C.: U.S. Government Printing Office.

Cheek, F. & Miller, M. (1982). *Prisoners of Life: A Study of Occupational Stress Among State Corrections Officers.* Washington, D.C.: AFSCME.

Cheek, F. & Miller, M. (1983). "The Experience of Stress For Correction Officers: A Double-Bind Theory of Correctional Stress." *Journal Of Criminal Justice* 11: 105 - 120.

Cherniss, C. (1980). *Staff Burnout - Job Stress in the Human Services.* Thousand Oaks, CA: Sage Publications.

Chien-Yang, L. (1991). "The Analysis of Job-Related Attitudes of Correctional Officers in Taiwan." Unpublished doctoral dissertation, Sam Houston State University.

Clemmer, D. (1958). *The Prison Community.* New York: Holt, Rinehart, and Winston.

Colvin, G.S. (n.d.). "Developing CERT in a Kentucky Jail." Retrieved on August 18, 2004 from http://.corrections.com/cert/column1.html

Corrections Corporation of America. (n.d.). "Our Customers Tell the Story." Retrieved January 13, 2003, from http://www.correctionscorp.com/main/client.html

Correctional Services Corporation. (2001). "Welcome." Retrieved January 13, 2003, from http://www.correctionalservices.com/default.html

Courtright, K.E. & Mackey, D.A. (2004) "Job Desirability Among Criminal Justice Majors: Exploring Relationships Between Personal Characteristics and Occupational Attractiveness." *Journal of Criminal Justice Education*, 15, 311 - 326.

Crary, D. (2001). "Bitterness,Resilience Coexist in Alabama's Segregated Prison Unit for HIV - Infected Inmates." Retrieved July 29, 2004, from http://www.sfgate.com/cgi-bin/article.cgi?file=/news/archive/2001/08/17national1314EDT0588.DTL&ty...

Crouch, B. (1985). "Pandora's Box: Women Guards in Men's Prisons." *Journal of Criminal Justice* 13: 535-548.

Crouch, B. & Alpert, G. (1982). "Sex and Occupational Socialization Among Prison Guards: A Longitudinal Study." *Criminal Justice and Behavior* 9: 159-176.

Cullen, F., Link, B., Cullen, J. , & Wolfe, N. (1989). "How Satisfying is Prison Work? A Comparative Occupational Approach." *Journal Of Offender Counseling, Services & Rehabilitation* 14: 89-108.

Cullen, F., Lutze, F., Link, B., & Wolfe, N. (1989) "The Correctional Orientation of Prison Guards: Do Officers Support Rehabilitation?" *Federal Probation* (March): 33-42.

Cullen, F., Link, B., Wolfe, N., & Frank, J. (1985). "The Social Dimensions of Correctional Officer Stress." *Justice Quarterly* 2: 505-528.

Dane County Sheriff's Department. (n.d.). "Homepage." Retrieved January 14, 2003, from http://www.co.dane.wi.us/shrf

Dean, D. (1961). "Alienation: Its Meaning and Measurement." *American Sociological Review* 26: 753-758.

Dempsey, J. S. & L.S. Frost (2005). *In Introduction to Policing* (3rd). Belmont, CA: West/Wadsworth Publishing Company.

DiIulio, J. J. Jr. (1987). *Governing Prisons: A Comparative Study of Correctional Management.* NY: The Free Press.

Duffee, D. & V. O'Leary (1986). "Formulating Correctional Goals: The Interaction of Environment, Belief, and Organizational Structure". In David Duffee (ed). *Correctional Management: Change & Control in Correctional Organizations.* Prospect Heights, Il.: Waveland Press.

Egrometrics' COVT. (n.d.). "Correction Officer Video Test." Retrieved January 13, 2003, from http://www.ergometrics.org/correct1.htm

Farkas, M. (1997). "The Normative Code Among Correctional Officers: An Exploration of Components and Functions." *Journal Of Crime And Justice* 20: 23 - 36.

Farmer, R. (1977). "Cynicism - A Factor in Corrections Work." *Journal of Criminal Justice* 4: 237-246.

Farnworth, M., Longmire, D. R., & West, V.M. (1998). "College Students' Views on Criminal Justice. *Journal of Criminal Justice Education*, 9, 39 - 58.

Federal Bureau of Prisons. (May, 2002). "Quick Facts." Retrieved September 30, 2002, from http://www.bop.gov/fact0598.html

Fisher, M., O"Brien, E., & Austern, D. (1987). *Practical Law for Jail and Prison Personnel.* Washington, D.C.: National Institute of Corrections.

Florida Department of Corrections. (n.d.). "Correctional Officer Employment Information." Retrieved April 8, 2002, from http://www.dc.state.fl.us/ employ/co.html

Florida Department Of Corrections. (n.d.). "2001-2002 Annual Report: Personnel." Retrieved January 23, 2003, from http://www.dc.state.fl.us/ pub/annual/0102/personnel.html

French, J. & Raven, B. (1959). "The Bases of Social Power." In D. Cartwright (Ed.), *Studies in Social Power.* Ann Arbor, MI: University of Michigan.

Fry, L., & Glaser, D. (1987). "Gender Differences in Work Adjustment of Prison Employees". *Journal of Offender Counseling Services and Rehabilitation* 12: 39-52.

Gagnon v. Scarpelli, 411 U.S. 778 (1973).

General Accounting Office. (1996). *Private and Public Prisons: Studies Comparing Operational Costs and/or Quality of Service.* GAO/GGD-96-158.

Glaze, L., & Palla, S. (2004). *Probation and Parole in the United States, 2003.* U.S. Department of Justice. NCJ 205336.

Gross, G., Larson, S., Urban, G., & Zupan, L. (1994). "Gender Differences in Occupational Stress Among Correctional Officers." *American Journal Of Criminal Justice* 18: 219-234.

Grossi, E ., & Berg, B. (1991). "Stress and Job Dissatisfaction Among Correctional Officers: An Unexpected Finding." *International Journal of Offender Therapy and Comparative Criminology* 35: 74 - 81.

Hammett, T. & Harmon, P. (1999a). "Sexually Transmitted Diseases and Hepatitis: Buren of Disease Among Inmates." In T.M. Hammett, et al. (Eds.), *1996 - 1997 Update: HIV/AIDS, STDs, and TB in Correctional Facilities.* Washington, D.C.: U.S. Department of Justice.

218

Hammett, T, & Harmon, P. (1999b). "HIV Transmission and Risk Factors, Precautionary and Preventive Measures." In T.M. Hammett, P. Harmon & L.M. Maruschak (Eds.), *1996-1997 Update: HIV/AIDS, STDs, and TB in Correctional Facilities* (pp. 47-52). Washington, D.C.: U.S. Department of Justice.

Hammett, T & Harmon, P. (1999c). "Tuberculosis." In T.M. Hammett, P. Harmon & L.M. Maruschak (Eds.), *1996-1997 Update: HIV/AIDS, STDs, and TB in Correctional Facilities* (pp. 85-91). Washington D.C: U.S. Department of Justice.

Haney, C., Banks, C, and Zimbardo, P. (1973). "Interpersonal Dynamics in a Simulated Prison". *International Journal of Criminology and Penology* 4: 207-209.

Heffernan, E. (1985). "A Note of the Origins of American Prisons." In R.M. Carter, et al. (Eds), *Correctional Institutions* (3rd ed). NY: Harper & Row, Publishers.

Hepburn, J. (1985). "The Exercise of Power in Coercive Organizations: A Study of Prison Guards". *Criminology* 23: 146-164.

Hepburn, J. (1987). "Prison Control Structure and Its Effects on Work Attitudes - The Perceptions and Attitudes of Prison Guards". *Journal of Criminal Justice* 15: 49-64.

Hepburn, J., & Albonetti, C. (1980) "Role Conflict in Correctional Institutions." *Criminology* 17: 455-459.

Hepburn, J., & Knepper, P. (1993). "Correctional Officers as Human Service Workers: The Effect on Job Satisfaction." *Justice Quarterly* 10: 315-335.

Hope v. Pelzer et al., 536 U.S. 730 (2002).

Horne, P. (1985). "Female Corrections Officers: A Status Report." *Federal Probation* 49: 46-54.

Hoult, T. (1969). *Dictionary of Modern Sociology.* Totowa, NJ: Littlefield-Adams.

Huang, F. (1993). "A Conceptual Examination of the Determinants of Occupational Attitudes of Jail Personnel in the Republic of China." Unpublished doctoral dissertation, Sam Houston State University.

Hudson v. McMillian et al., 503 U.S. 1 (1992).

Hurst, T., & Hurst, M. (1997). "Gender Differences in Mediation of Severe Occupational Stress Among Correctional Officers". *American Journal of Criminal Justice* 22: 121-137.

Idaho Department of Corrections. (n.d.). "Community Corrections Offices: About Us." Retrieved September 8, 2004, from:http://www.corr.state.id.us/our_facilities/community.htm.

Irwin, J. (1980). *Prisons in Turmoil*. Boston: Little Brown.

Ives, G. (1970). *A History of Penal Methods*. Montclair, NJ: Patterson Smith.

Jackson v. Bishop, 404 F.2nd 571, 599 (1968).

Jackson, J. & Ammen, S. (1996). "Race and Correctional Officers' Punitive Attitudes Toward Treatment Programs For Inmates." *Journal Of Criminal Justice* 24, 153-166.

Jacobs, J. (1977). *Stateville: The Penitentiary in Mass Society*. Chicago: The University of Chicago Press.

Jacobs, J. (1981) "The Sexual Integration of the Prison's Guard Force: A Few Comments on Dothard v. Rawlinson." In R. Ross (Ed.) *Prison Guard/ Correctional Officer: The Use and Abuse of Human Resources of Prisons*. Toronto: Butterworth.

Jacobs, J. (1978). "What Prison Guards Think - A Profile of the Illinois Force." *Crime and Delinquency* 24: 185-196.

Jacobs, J, & Kraft, L. (1978). "Integrating the Keepers: A Comparison of Black and White Prison Guards in Illinois". *Social Problems* 25: 304-318.

Jacobs, J., & Retsky, H. (1980) "Prison Guard" In B. Crouch (Ed.) *The Keepers*. Springfield, IL: Charles Thomas Publishers.

Jacobs, J., & Grear, M. (1978). "Drop Outs and Rejects - An Analysis of the Prison Guard's Revolving Door." *Criminal Justice Review* 2: 57-70.

Johnson, R. (1997). "Race, Gender, and the American Prison: Historical Observations. In J. Pollock (Ed.), *Prisons Today and Tomorrow.* Gaithersburg, MD: Aspen Publishers, Inc.

Johnson, R. (1996). *Hard Time: Understanding and Reforming the Prison.* Belmont, CA: Wadsworth Publishing Co.

Josi, D. & Sechrest, D. (1998). *The Changing Career of the Correctional Officer: Policy Implications for the 21st Century.* Boston: Butterworth-Heinemann.

Jurik, N. (1985a). "Individual and Organizational Determinants of Correctional Officer Attitude Toward Inmates". *Criminology* 23, 523-539.

Jurik, N. (1985b). "An Officer and a Lady: Organizational Barriers to Women Working as Correctional Officers in Men's Prisons." *Social Problems* 32: 375-388.

Jurik, N.C. & Halemba, G. J. (1984). "Gender, Working Condition s and the Job Satisfaction of Women in a Non-Traditional Occupation: Female Correctional Officers in Men's Prisons." *Sociological Quarterly* 25, 551-566.

Jurik, N., Halemba, G., Musheno, M., & Boyle, B. (1987). "Educational Attainment, Job Satisfaction, and the Professionalization of Correctional Officers." *Work and Occupations* 14: 106 - 125.

Jurik, N., & Winn, R. (1987). "Describing Correctional-Security Dropouts and Rejects - An Individual or Organizational Profile?" *Criminal Justice and Behavior* 14: 5-25.

Kansas Department of Corrections. (2002). "2002 Corrections Briefing Report, January, 2002. " Retrieved January 23, 2003, from http://docnet.dc.state. ks.us

Kamerman, J. (1995). "Correctional Officer Suicide". *The Keeper's Voice* 16: 7-8.

Kauffman, K. (1981). "Prison Officers Attitudes and Perceptions of Attitudes" A Case of Pluralistic Ignorance". *Journal of Research in Crime and Delinquency* 18: 272-294.

Kauffman, K. (1988). *Prison Officers and Their World.* London: Harvard University Press.

Kentucky Corrections. (n.d.). "Probation & Parole." Retrieved September 8, 2004, from: http://www.corrections.ky.gov/P&P.htm.

Kinsell, L., & Sheldon, R. (1981) "Survey of Correctional Officers at a Medium Security Prison." *Corrections Today* 43: 40-43.

Kissel, P., & Katsampes, P. (1980). "The Impact of Women Corrections Officers on the Functioning of Institutions Housing Male Inmates." *Journal of Offender Counseling, Services, and Rehabilitation* 4: 213-231.

Klofas, J. (1984). "Reconsidering Prison Personnel: New Views of the Correctional Officer Subculture." *International Journal of Offender Therapy and Comparative Criminology* 28: 169-175.

Klofas, J. (1986). "Discretion Among Correctional Officers: The Influence of Urbanization, Age and Race." *International Journal of Offender Therapy and Comparative Criminology* 30: 111-124.

Klofas, J. & Toch, H. (1982). "The Guard Subculture Myth". *Journal of Research in Crime and Delinquency* 19: 238-254.

Knight. K., & Saylor, W. (1991). "Male and Female Employees' Perception of Prison Work: Is there a Difference?" *Justice Quarterly* 8: 505-524.

Lasky, G., Gordon, C., & Srebalus, D. (1986). "Occupational Stressors Among Federal Correctional Officers Working in Different Security Levels." *Criminal Justice and Behavior* 13, 317-327.

Lawrence, R., & Mahan, S. (1998). "Women Corrections Officers in Men's Prisons: Acceptance and Perceived Job Performance". *Women and Criminal Justice* 9: 63-86.

Lekkerkerker, E. (1931). *Reformatories for Women in the United States.* New York: J.B. Wolters.

Legace, D. (1994). "Acceptance of Female Correctional Officers in Institutions for Men: A Canadian Perspective." Unpublished master's thesis, Saint Mary's University.

Lombardo, L. (1985). "Group Dynamics and the Prison Guard Subculture: Is the Subculture an Impediment to Helping Inmates?" *International Journal of Offender Therapy and Comparative Criminology* 29: 79-90.

Lombardo, L. (1989). *Guards Imprisoned Correctional Officers at Work* (2nd ed.). Cincinnati, OH: Anderson Publishing.

Marquart, J. (1986). "Prison Guards and the Use of Physical Coercion as a Mechanism of Prisoner Control". *Criminology* 24: 347-366.

Massachusetts Correction Officer Federated Union. (n.d.) "Welcome." Retrieved April 23, 2003, from http://www.mcofu.com/start_page. htm.

Mecham, L.R. (2004). "2003 Judicial Business: Annual Report of the Director." Administrative Office of the U.S. Courts Washington, D.C. Retrieved September 2, 2004 from www.uscourts.gov

Merlak, S., & Hepburn, J. (1992). "Job Satisfaction, Stress, and Burnout Among Correctional Officers: A Multivariate Analysis". Paper presented at the annual meeting of the Academy of Criminal Justice Sciences, Pittsburg, PA.

Morris, N. & Hawkins, G. (1970). *The Honest Politician's Guide to Crime Control.* Chicago: The University of Chicago Press.

Morrissey v. Brewer, 408 U.S. 471 (1972).

Muir, W. (1977). *Police: Streetcorner Politicians.* Chicago: University of Chicago Press.

New Mexico Department of Corrections. (n.d.). "Probation and Parole Division." Retrieved on September 8, 2004, from http://corrections.state.nm.us/ parole/intro.html

North Carolina Department of Corrections. (n.d.). "Division of Community Corrections." Retrieved on September 8, 2004, from: http://www.doc. state.nc.us/dcc/index.htm.

Maruschak, L. M. (2004). *HIV in Prisons, 2001*. U.S. Department of Justice NCJ 202293.

National Institute of Corrections. (n.d.). "About NIC." Retrieved January 13, 2003, from http://www.nicic.org

New York City Department of Corrections. (n.d.). "Department Overview." Retrieved January 14, 2003, from http://www.nyc.gov/html/doc/ overview.html

North Carolina Department of Corrections. (n.d.). "Careers in Corrections." Retrieved April 8, 2002, from http://www.doc.state.nc.us/career/jobs.htm

North Carolina Department of Corrections. (n.d.). "History of the North Carolina Prison System." Retrieved on April 8, 2002, from http://www .oc.state.nc.us/admin/page1.htm

National Institute of Allergy and Infectious Diseases. (2003). "HIV Infection and AIDS: An Overview." Retrieved on July 27, 2004, from http:// www.niaid. hih.gov/factsheets/ hivinf.htm

Office of Probation and Pretrial Services. (2003). "Court & Community: An Information Series about U.S. Probation and Pretrial Services : Probation Officers." Retrieved on September 24, 2004, from http://www.uscourts. gov/misc/2003-probation.PDF.

Oklahoma Department of Corrections. (2004). "Tuberculosis Control Program. Policy- OP 140301 Effective Date 5/12/04. " Retrieved on August 11, 2004, from http:// www.doc.state.ok.us/ Offtech/op140301.htm

Oklahoma Department of Corrections. (2003). "Use of Force Standards and Reportable Incidents OP- 050108 Effective Date 4/21/03." Retrieved on August 27, 2004, from http://www. doc. state.us/Offtech/op050108.htm

Ohio Department of Rehabilitation and Corrections. (n.d.). "Ohio Corrections Assessment Center." Retrieved April 5, 2002, from http: / www.drc.state. oh.us/web/ocac.htm

Oklahoma Department of Corrections Training Administration. (n.d.). "Welcome." Retrieved April 8, 2002, from http://www.doc.state.ok.us/ training/cotrain.htm

Owen, B. (1985). "Race and Gender Relations Among Prison Workers." *Crime and Delinquency* 31: 147-158.

Parisi, N. (1984). "The Female Correctional Officer: Her Progress Toward and Prospects for Equality." *The Prison Journal* 64: 92-109.

Patenaude, A., & Golden, J. (2000). "Is Race a Factor in Saying "I Ain't Working Here No More": Exploring Retention Among Arkansas Correctional Officers." *Corrections Management Quarterly* 4, 64 -74.

Peterson, C. (1982). "Doing Time with the Boys: An Analysis of Women Correctional Officers in All-Male Facilities. In B. Price & N. Sokoloff (Eds.) *The Criminal Justice and Women: Women Offenders, Victims, Workers.* New York: Clark Boardman Company.

Philliber, S. (1987). "Thy Brother's Keeper: A Review of the Literature on Correctional Officers." *Justice Quarterly* 4: 9-36.

Poole, E. & Regoli, R. (1980a). "Role Stress, Custody Orientation, and Disciplinary Practices". *Criminology* 18: 225-236

Poole, E., & Regoli, R. (1980b). "Work Relations and Cynicism Among Prison Guards." *Criminal Justice and Behavior* 7: 303-314..

Poole, E. & Regoli, R. (1981). "Alienation in Prisons: An Examination of the Work Relationships of Prison Guards." *Criminology* 19: 251-270.

Poole, E., & Regoli, R. (1983). "Professionalism, Role Conflict, Work Alienation, and Anomia: A Look at Prison Management." *The Social Science Journal* 20: 63-70.

Poole, E., & Pogrebin, M. (1987). "Judicial Intervention and Work Alienation - A Study of Jail Guards". *Howard Journal of Criminal Justice* 26: 217-231.

Pollock, J. (1997). *Prisons Today and Tomorrow*. Gaithersburg, MD.:Aspen Publishers, Inc.

Purkiss, M., Kifer, K., Hemmens, C., & Burton, V. (2003) "Probation Officer Functions- A Statutory Analysis." [Electronic Version]. *Federal Probation* 67: 12-23.

Robinson, D., Porporino, F., & Simourd, L. (1993). "The Influence of Career Orientation on Support for Rehabilitation Among Correctional Officers." *The Prison Journal* 73: 162-177.

Rogers, R. (1991). "The Effects of Educational Level on Correctional Officer Job Satisfaction." *Journal of Criminal Justice* 19: 123-137.

Reaves, B. & Hart, T. (2001). *Federal Law Enforcement Officers, 2000.* Washington, D.C.: U.S. Department of Justice.

Reaves, B. & Hickman, M. (2001). *Sheriffs' Offices, 1999.* Washington, D.C.: U.S. Department of Justice.

Reaves, B. & Bauer, M. (2003). *Federal Law Enforcement Officers, 2002.* Washington, D.C.: U.S. Department of Justice.

Robinson, D., Porporino, F., & Simourd, L. (1993). "The Influence of Career Orientation on Support for Rehabilitation Among Correctional Staff." *The Prison Journal* 73: 162-177.

Rosecrance, J. (1987). "A Typology of Presentence Probation Investigators." *International Journal of Offender Therapy and Comparative Criminology* 31: 163-177.

Ross, D. (1996). "An Assessment of Prisoner Assaults on Corrections Officers." *Corrections Compendium* 21: 6-10.

Rowan, J. (1996). *More Female Correctional Officers Mean Fewer Assaults Overall: Another Myth Debunked.* Roseville, MN: Criminal and Juvenile Justice International.

Ruffin v. Commonwealth of Virginia, 62 Va. (21 Gratt) 790 (1871).

Sandu, H. (1972). "Perceptions of Prison Guards: A Cross-National Study of India and Canada." *International Review of Modern Sociology* 2: 26-32.

Seeman, R. (1959). "On the Meaning of Alienation." *American Sociological Review* 24: 783-791.

Seiter, R., & West, A. (2003). "Supervision Styles in Probation and Parole: An Analysis of Activities." *Journal Of Offender Rehabilitation* 38: 57 - 75.

226

Shamir, B. & Drory, A. (1981). "Some Correlates of Prison Guards' Beliefs". *Criminal Justice and Behavior* 8: 233-249.

Shamir, B. & Drory, A. (1982). "Occupational Tedium Among Correctional Officers". *Criminal Justice and Behavior* 9: 79-99.

Simpson, S. & White, M. (1985). "The Female Guard in the All-Male Prison." In I. Moyer (Ed.) *The Changing Roles of Women in the Criminal Justice System: Offenders, Victims and Professionals.* Prospect Heights, IL: Waveland Press.

Skolnick, J. (1966). *Justice Without Trial.* New York: Wiley.

Smith, C., & Hepburn, J. (1979). "Alienation in Prison Organizations". *Criminology* 17: 251- 262.

Snell, T. (2001). *Capital Punishment 2000.* U.S. Department of Justice NCJ-190598.

Specwarnte.com. (n.d.). "Connecticut Department of Correction Special Operations Unit." Retrieved August 18, 2004, from http://www. specwarnet.com/taclink/Corrections/ CT_DOC_ SOU.htm.

Special Operations. Com. (n.d.). "Federal Bureau of Prisons Special Operations and Response Teams (SORT)." Retrieved August 18, 2004, from http:// www.specialoperations.com/ Domestic/BOP/

Stephan. J. J. (1999). *State Prison Expenditures, 1996.* U.S. Department of Justice. NCJ 172211.

Stojkovic, S. (1990). "Accounts of Prison Work: Correctional Officers' Portrayals of Their Work Worlds". In G. Miller & J. Holstein (Eds), *Perspectives on Social Problems.* Greenwich, CT: Jai Press.

Sykes, G. (1958). *The Society of Captives - A Study of a Maximum Security Prison.* Princeton, NJ: Princeton University Press.

Sykes, G., & Messenger, S. (1960). "The Inmate Social System". In R. Cloward et al., *Theoretical Studies in Social Organization of the Prison.* New York: Social Science Research Council.

Szockyj, E. (1989). "Working in a Man's World: Women Correctional Officers in an Institution for Men." *Canadian Journal of Criminology* 31: 319-328.

Tennessee v. Garner, 471 U.S. 1 (1985)

Teske, R, and Williamson, H. (1979). " Correctional Officers' Attitudes Toward Selected Treatment Programs". *Criminal Justice and Behavior* 6: 59-66.

Texas Department of Criminal Justice. (n.d.). "Institutional Division." Retrieved April 5, 2002, from http://www.tdcj.state.tx.us/id/id-home.htm.

Texas Department of Criminal Justice. (n.d.). "Correctional Officer." Retrieved April 5, 2002, from http://www.tdcj.state.tx.us/vacancy/COinfo/empco. htm

The President's Commission on Law Enforcement and Administration of Justice. (1967). *Task Force Report: Corrections.* Washington, D.C.: U.S. Government Printing Office.

Topham, J.H. (n.d.). "Correctional Response Teams - 5 Officer Cell Extraction." Retrieved August 18, 2004, from http://www.corrections.com/ cert/ topham1.html

TreatHIV.com. (n.d.). "Your Health Risk in Correctional Settings." Retrieved July 28, 2004, from http://www.treathiv.com/4patient_edu/4.11.1.cos. html

Toch, H., & Klofas, J. (1982) "Alienation and a Desire for Job Enrichment Among Correctional Officers." *Federal Probation Quarterly* 1: 35-44.

United States Department of Justice. (2001). "National Correctional Population Reaches New High Grows by 126,4000 during 2000 to total 6.5 Million Adults." Press Release August, 2001

UNAIDS. (2004). "2004 Report on the Global AIDS Epidemic: Executive Summary." Retrieved August 2, 2004, from http: //www. unaids.org/ bangkok2004/ GAR2004_pdf/ GAR2004_ Execsumm _en.pdf.

United States Department of Health and Human Service. (1995). *Controlling TB in Correctional Facilities.* Atlanta, GA: Centers for Disease Control and Prevention.

228

United States Probation and Pretrial Services System Year in Review Report. (2003). *Fiscal Year 2002*. Prepared by the Office of Probation and Pretrial Services, Administrative Office of the United States Courts in cooperation with the Chiefs Advisory Group.

Van Voorhis, P., Cullen, F., Link, B., & Wolfe, N. (1991). "The Impact of Race and Gender on Correctional Officers' Orientation to the Integrated Environment." *Journal of Research in Crime and Delinquency* 28: 472-500.

Walters, S. (1996a). "The Determinants of Job Satisfaction Among Canadian and American Correctional Officers". *Journal of Crime and Justice* 23: 45-53.

Walters, S. (1996b). "Across the Border: A Comparison of U.S. And Canadian Correctional Officers". *Journal of Offender Rehabilitation* 23: 185-195.

Walters, S. (1995). "The Custody Orientation of Correctional Officers: An International Comparison." *International Journal Of Comparative And Applied Criminal Justice* 19, 61-71.

Walters, S. (1993a). "Changing the Guard: Male Correctional Officers' Attitudes Toward Women as Co-Workers." *Journal of Offender Rehabilitation* 20: 47-60.

Walters, S. (1993b). "Gender, Job Satisfaction and Correctional Officers: A Comparative Analysis." *The Justice Professional* 7, 22-33.

Walters, S. (1992a). "Attitudinal and Demographic Differences Between Male and Female Correctional Officers: A Study in Three Midwestern Prisons." *Journal of Offender Rehabilitation* 18: 173-189.

Walters, S. (1992b). [Correctional Officer Survey.] Unpublished raw data.

Walters, S. (1991). "Alienation and the Correctional Officer: A Multivariate Analysis." *American Journal of Criminal Justice* 16: 50-62.

Walters, S. (1988). "Correctional Officers' Perceptions of Powerlessness." *Journal of Crime and Justice* 11: 47-59.

Walters, S. (1986). *Alienation, Powerlessness, and Social Isolation Among Correctional Officers.* Unpublished doctoral dissertation, University of Montana.

Walters, S. (1985). [Correctional Officer Survey.] Unpublished raw data.

Walters, S., & Lagace, D. (1999). "Gender Difference in Occupational Characteristics of Canadian Correctional Officers." *International Journal of Comparative and Applied Criminal Justice* 23: 45-53.

Webb, G. and Morris, D. (1978). *Prison Guards - The Culture and Perspective of an Occupational Group.* Austin, TX: Coker Books.

Whitehead, J. & Lindquist, C. (1986). "Correctional Officers' Job Burnout: A Path Model." *Journal of Research in Crime and Delinquency* 23: 23-42.

Whitehead, J., Linquist, C, & Klofas, J. (1987). "Correctional Officer Professional Orientation: A Replication of the Klofas - Toch Measure." *Criminal Justice and Behavior* 14, 468-486.

Whitehead, J. & Lindquist, C. (1989). "Determinants of Correctional Officers' Professional Orientation". *Justice Quarterly* 6: 69-87.

Weinbaum, C., Lyerla, R & Margolis. H. (2003). "Prevention and Control of Infections with Hepatitis Viruses in Correctional Settings." Centers for Disease Controls. Morbidity and Morality Weekly Report Volume 53, January, 2003.

Westley, W. (1970). *Violence and the Police - A Sociological Study of Law, Custom, and Morality.* Cambridge, MA: MIT Press.

Wicks, R. (1980). *Guard! Society's Professional Prisoner.* Houston: Gulf Publishing Company.

Whitely et al. v. Albers, 475 U.S. 312 (1986).

Williams, T. (1983). "Custody and Conflict: An Organizational Study of Prison Officers' Roles and Attitudes." *Australian and New Zealand Journal of Criminology* 16: 44-55.

230

Williams, T. & Soutar, G. (1984). "Levels of Custody and Attitude Differences Among Prison Officers: A Comparative Study." *Australian and New Zealand Journal of Criminology* 17: 87-89.

Wisconsin Administrative Rules. Chapter DOC 306; "Security."

Zimmer, L. (1986). *Women Guarding Men.* Chicago: The University of Chicago Press.

Zupan, L. (1986). "Gender-Related Differences in Correctional Officers' Perceptions and Attitudes". *Journal of Criminal Justice* 4: 349-361.

INDEX

234